God Bless

Turner

Joyce

Pain Through A Child's Eyes

Joyce Turner

authorHOUSE®

AuthorHouse™
1663 Liberty Drive
Bloomington, IN 47403
www.authorhouse.com
Phone: 1-800-839-8640

First published by AuthorHouse   1/28/2011

ISBN: 978-1-4567-2247-0 (sc)
ISBN: 978-1-4567-2249-4 (hc)
ISBN: 978-1-4567-2249-4 (e)

Library of Congress Control Number: 2011900170

Printed in the United States of America

This book is printed on acid-free paper.

Certain stock imagery © Thinkstock.

This book is dedicated to the many family members who encouraged me to place on paper what was in my heart, to help others who are experiencing pain and hurt, both now and in the past. Also, I would especially like to dedicate this book to my two granddaughters, Taran and Jordan. Taran pushed me until it was completed and both she and Jordan were willing to be pictured in my book. Taran is on the front cover and Jordan is pictured throughout the book. They both are very special as are all my grandchildren.

ACKNOWLEDGEMENTS

I would like to acknowledge my husband, George, who has given me a life filled with answered dreams, a Christian home, and a life dedicated to our marriage. He is a good man!

Contents

INTRODUCTION

This book is based on a true story of the life of a child Joyce, who was the victim of cruel circumstances that led to years of rejection, pain, heartache, and abuse. Her blue eyes saw more in her young life than most see in a lifetime. She felt she would always be a product of her past and could never see any way to a brighter future. Shame and disgrace had taken a toll on her young life, heart, and soul. She had lost so much hope as a result of her pain and struggles at a tender young age that she contemplated suicide on many occasions. Her life seemed to be spiraling down a slippery slope of no return. Each day she stared into a mirror at a pale reflection of emptiness that gave her no reason to live or have hope for a brighter tomorrow. Her heart-wrenching home situation of abuse, lack of love, insecurity, and turmoil drove her into a deep anger that almost destroyed her life. Her world was shaken and turned upside down, and she felt there was no one she could turn to for help or advice. Yet something deep inside continually nudged her along the way to continue her fight for survival. It took an extreme amount of energy to push the mess of life and the tears of rejection out of sight in order to maintain her sanity. Nevertheless, she would finally see light at the end of that dark tunnel of destruction that had taken place years earlier.

The longing in Joyce's tender heart for a better tomorrow was a driving force that would keep her from abandoning all hope. *Pain through a Child's Eyes* is a story that will touch the very core of your heart and bring tears to your eyes as you feel the pain her blue eyes and heart encountered. Nevertheless, as you read about the journey that Joyce's painful life took, you will also feel the overwhelming hope, peace and love she found in her future.

Names have been changed to protect the privacy of others. Accounts of written material are the view seen through the eyes of a young child who only wanted to be accepted and loved, but who seemed always to be the recipient of abuse, heartache, and pain. Accounts of events before Joyce was born were taken from conversations with family members and friends. My hope is that reading this book will encourage you never to give up on yourself or cave in to the pain of circumstances that have invaded your life. You have within you the courage to push past your circumstances to a brighter tomorrow, if you will only believe.

CHAPTER I

Death in a Ravine

My mother, Linda, was born to Grandpa and Grandma Smith as a premature baby weighing only two and a half pounds. In those days, babies born premature and at that weight had little to no chance of survival; however, Mother was a fighter, and somehow she survived. Grandma Smith talked about how small she was.

"I had to carry your Mommy around on a pillow because she was so fragile and small," she would say. Grandma Smith was afraid to place her in a big crib because she was much too small. A dresser drawer would be her bed. She would be the youngest girl of the ten children Grandma Smith gave birth to. Mother never seemed to be her parents' favorite daughter, judging from their negative actions when she was around. She just didn't seem to measure up to their expectation for a daughter.

Mother was a teenage girl when she met a young man named Luke and fell in love. Luke was handsome by all accounts. Marriage was in their plans, some said. Back in those days, it was an exciting time if a girl was married at a young age. You were called an old maid if you were not married by the time you were sixteen! So marriage was strong on the minds of every young girl in those days, and they were always looking for their soul mates. Mother was well past sixteen, and I guess she felt her biological clock was ticking away! But, at last, she had met Luke and they were in love.

1

Everything seemed to be going great, and Mother was happy and looking forward to a bright future. However, something dark and painful was lurking at the bottom of a dark ravine. Mother's sweetheart, Luke, was on his way to pick her up for a date. She was excited. However, that dark, dusty road to her house was holding a pain that would pierce Mother's very heart.

Luke, the young man she loved, had a tragic accident. The report from those who saw the accident was that Luke was driving much too fast and lost control of the car. Though he tried as hard as he could to recover, the loose gravel would show no mercy for a young man who was soon to be married. He plunged down an embankment into a dark, cold ravine, and his life ended. His mangled car and body were almost beyond recognition, by all accounts.

When word reached Mother, she was devastated. She really didn't believe the words she was hearing, and she was in denial that they were true. However, reality soon hit her like a ton of bricks, and she realized she was alone and carrying a dark secret. Frightened and confused, Mother tried to hide the fact that she was pregnant with her first child. That first child was my sister, Deborah. Mother did a great job of hiding it, everyone said. Until one day mother was found screaming with labor pains in the barn loft, no one knew that she was "with child!"

That was the day her forbidden sin was exposed to her family and friends. Everyone said that Grandma and Grandpa Smith were surprised and mad at the same time. She gave birth to my older sister, Deborah, alone and without her first love. Grandpa and Grandma Smith had no compassion for their youngest daughter. They always told her, "You made this bed of trouble, now you will have to deal with the consequences."

Their attitude of hard-core discipline left no room for tolerating such a mistake or feeling compassion for a young girl who months earlier had lost her first love. Mother would have to face shame and disgrace alone, with no one to hold her in their loving arms. The results of her actions would make her the black sheep of the family.

She lived day after day with the memory of what could have been. Her eyes would reflect the hurt and pain she felt in her heart as she tried to move forward. Because of the difficulty she was facing, Luke's parents decided to take in Deborah as their own. However, shortly after Deborah moved in with Luke's family, Mother and her family decided to move far away to another town at the foot of the Blue Ridge Mountains. Mother wasn't willing to leave Deborah behind with Luke's family, so she, too, would move to the new town. This could mean a second chance for Mother to start a new life, if she would take advantage of the opportunity. However, because of the deep hurt that seemed to linger in her very soul, what could have been her second chance would only materialize into more self-destruction, pain, and rejection.

Chapter 2

Left Behind

Mother met Roger, my father, after moving to a small rural farm. I really have no idea how they met. She never said much about Roger when I was a young child, nor did she say much about him after I became an adult. They married, and she became pregnant with her second child. That child was me, Joyce. Nevertheless, trouble seemed to be on the horizon for this young couple.

The story is that she and Roger had extreme difficulty in their marriage. That difficulty eventually would mean death to their marriage. No one would reveal any details of what had really happened, nor would they discuss it in my presence. It seemed painful for Mother, and I never knew Roger well enough to ask. Maybe it was because Mother was still in love with Luke, the young man who had lost his life one night in a ravine many years earlier. She never seemed happy after the incident. Mother was a troubled young lady, and no one really knew what driving force was pushing her into a life of pain, hurt, and unhappiness. She always seemed to be looking for something to fill the emptiness that was driving her further and further down a road of pain and hurt. It seemed that if there was a rough spot in the road she was traveling, she would be sure to hit it.

She was a child who had had to fight for her life since the day she was born, and she continued that fight as she became an adult. She never seemed to find what she was looking for to fill the void she carried deep down in her soul. The marriage came to an end, and a rejected young lady was set out in front of her parents' farmhouse one late afternoon. Pregnant, rejected, and humiliated, she would yet again have to depend on her parents for her livelihood and for a roof over her head. Mother stood and gazed into the distance as Roger departed, fading away into the dust that rose behind his car. It appeared he never looked back at the woman who was carrying his child.

She entered the house rejected, pregnant, and alone once again. Sitting down in a chair, she buried her face in her hands, weeping bitterly from another broken heart. She was faced with bearing another child on her own, with no support from the man she thought would be her partner forever. Life had, yet again, dished out more pain and hurt for a young lady looking for her soul mate! Her destiny always seemed to take her to a dead end road and a heart broken by rejection. Would she ever love again?

CHAPTER 3

Rejected in the Womb

Those stormy nights started before I was ever born. After being left behind by Roger, Mother would, yet again, have to deal with the rejection of Grandpa and Grandma Smith. Roger had left behind an unborn child and a rejected wife to build another life without support and love. I was rejected in the womb by a father who just years earlier had promised to honor and love his wife until death separated them. He seemed to have forgotten those vows.

Rejection took place before I took my first breath and gave that loud cry of life. My life began on a farm, surrounded by the eyes of those who would have preferred that I not be born. As far back as I can remember, my grandparents treated me just as another mouth to feed and an additional child underfoot. I never knew as a child why it seemed I was an inconvenience to everyone in my family. The feelings of rejection would invade my young life and bring insecurities so deeply rooted that it would take many, many years to overcome. I was abandoned by those who should have held a young, blue-eyed girl in their arms. Could they not feel the heartache, suffering, and pain that flowed from this child's pale, rejected face? I had more weight on my shoulders at four than most have at forty.

My grandparents' constant reminders that I had a mother and father who somehow felt no obligation or responsibility for the child they birthed echoed into my tender heart and ears. Rejection would invade my life like water from a broken dam after a dark, stormy night. Dream after dream was shattered like a broken windowpane. Would this innocent, blue-eyed child survive her surroundings? Would she ever feel loved and wanted by those around her?

As I look back to the rejection and emptiness my mother seemed to constantly project on her face and in her actions, I realize that the same feelings of rejection were handed down to another generation. I have always heard that what affects a mother when she is pregnant will also affect the baby in her womb. I don't know how true that is; however, I do know that my road to rejection started in the womb when my father drove away, rejecting any contact with his unborn child. The bitter feelings of rejection would linger with me for many, many years. Would there be any hope of recovery from a rejected heart? Only time would tell.

CHAPTER 4

Stranger

Roger only visited me twice that I can remember in my lifetime. I simply don't remember much about him. He remarried and moved on with his life, leaving the responsibility of caring for me to someone else. Rejection from men would prove to be a pattern I would have to overcome.

The first time I remember seeing him, I was around four years old. It was a hot Saturday afternoon, and I was sitting on the front porch with Grandpa and Grandma Smith. We could see dust rising from the dirt road we lived on, so we knew someone was coming for a visit. There wasn't much traffic on the road and few people had cars, so we thought it must be someone special.

The car pulled into the front yard. Out stepped a strange man and woman. Grandpa and Grandma Smith had astonished looks on their faces.

"What you here for?" Grandpa Smith asked.

"I've come to see Joyce," the strange man replied. I could feel fear rising inside of me. I jumped up and hid behind Grandma Smith's chair. Who was this man? I kept my distance from the strange man as I peeped around Grandma Smith's chair with curiosity. My eyes studied him carefully. As I continued to stare around the chair, Grandma Smith invited them to sit on the front porch while they continued their conversation. What in the world did she mean, inviting them to sit on the porch? I was still seated halfway behind Grandma Smith's chair, not willing to get within reaching distance of these strange people Grandma Smith had for some reason invited to sit down! Was she out of her mind? I wondered. Who were they?

Grandpa Smith inquired, with a little suspicion in his voice, "Tell me why, after all these years, you have shown up to see Joyce."

"I really want to be a part of her life, and my wife and I would like to take her home with us for the weekend," the strange man replied.

"I don't know about you taking her home with you," said Grandpa Smith. He glanced over at Grandma Smith with questioning eyes. Grandma Smith looked at me sitting behind her chair. My wide blue eyes showed questions and fear as Grandma Smith turned away from me and continued to talk with this stranger. Who was he, and why did he want to take me away from the security of my grandparents' home? As the conversation continued, fear of what was going to happen next filled my heart. I needed to do something—and quick, before Grandma Smith decided to let me go!

With caution, I managed to get up and slip to the corner of the house, which I peered around just enough to see this strange man. I needed to run and hide before the stranger could talk Grandma Smith into letting me go home with him! But where was I to go? I crouched down on my knees and began crawling to the edge of the cornfield that was to the left of the house.

Running to the end of the row of corn that led to the barn, I ducked beneath the fence that separated them. Ripping my dress on the barbed-wire fence didn't slow me down, even if it did mean I would more than likely receive a whipping once Grandma Smith found out. Reaching the barn would give me refuge, I thought.

I continued hiding behind anything I could find. I crouched down on my hands and knees again until I reached the safety of the back of the barn. I was out of the sight and reach of that strange man now! But where should I go next? Should I hide in the barn loft? No, Grandpa Smith would for sure find me there. How about the wagon under the corncrib shed? No, that wouldn't be a good hiding place either. I looked around in desperation. *I know*, I told myself. I would go to Aunt Bell's house. They surely wouldn't find me there. I slipped from behind the barn, crouching down as far as I could, away from the eyes of those strange people. However, just when I thought I was free and clear, I heard Grandma Smith coming around the corner of the barn calling my name. Oh no! What could I do? I took off running as hard as I could down the road. The only thing visible was my cotton-top blond hair, which appeared each time I jumped over something in my way. I ran across the little stream to Aunt Bell's house as my heart pounded like a drum. I could hear Grandma Smith calling even louder, but I didn't slow down or look back. Running like a mad dog, I finally reached the security of Aunt Bell's house.

Hearing me out of breath and crying, Aunt Bell came out of the house to see what all the commotion was about. I told her about the strange man who was trying to take me home with him.

"Child, stop your crying, that's your father," Aunt Bell said.

My father? I thought to myself. *I've never seen this man before in my life!* My cousins started teasing me about having to go home with him. The more they teased, the more afraid I became. As I stood in Aunt Bell's yard, I saw that same car coming up the road to her house. Oh no! The strange man they were calling my father had followed me to Aunt Bell's house! In desperation, I ran to the back side of the house. Where would I go now to hide? I noticed a hole in the lattice that surrounded the bottom of Aunt Bell's house. Slipping through the hole in the lattice and crawling back under the house gave me a feeling of safety. However, fear was lingering in my heart, and I sobbed uncontrollably as I shook like a leaf in a summer storm.

The car pulled into Aunt Bell's driveway. I could hear the strange man talking to Aunt Bell. Then I heard Grandma Smith's voice. Oh no! Grandma Smith was with him! She would for sure drag me out from under the house and give me a whipping I would never forget. I heard footsteps coming in my direction. I inched back a little farther under the house. Grandma Smith bent down and looked straight into my sobbing blue eyes, trying to coax me out from under the house, but I wouldn't budge. The strange man Aunt Bell had called my father also bent down and began talking to me. I moved farther away from the hole in the lattice by crawling on my stomach. This gave me the secure feeling that I was out of his reach.

"Please, Joyce, I am not going to hurt you. If you don't want to go with me, I will not make you go. Just please come out and let me say good-bye to you," said the stranger they called my father.

Still fearful and sobbing, I replied. "I am not coming out until you leave. I don't want to go with you, and I don't want to tell you good-bye, so go away and leave me alone." The strange man looked sad, and his expression was filled with hurt and disappointment. Nevertheless, as far as I was concerned he could leave and never come back. He had never been a part of my life, and I sure didn't want to be a part of his life now! I watched as he slowly got up from the ground with sadness on his face.

"I am leaving now; you can come out," he said.

"No!" I replied. "I won't come out until you leave." I could hear him talking to Grandma Smith and Aunt Bell.

Because I was so far under the house, I could not hear them clearly. I knew one thing for sure: it was about me! However, I wasn't curious enough to come out from under the house to hear what they were saying. My hope was that the strange man would leave and never look back, as he had done years earlier before I was born.

He returned to the car with Grandma Smith by his side. Hearing the car door open gave me the courage to crawl closer to the opening in the lattice. Then silence filled the air, and I could see that Grandma Smith was getting into the car with the stranger. *He must be driving her back to the farmhouse,* I thought. The car door slammed. I moved closer to the hole in the lattice. He started the car and backed out of the driveway. I moved and positioned myself so I could see him drive down the hot, dusty road that led away from Aunt Bell's house. Cautiously, I fixed my eyes on the car until it was out of sight.

The dust began to rise on the road that led to Grandma Smith's house. He was taking her home. I could breathe a little easier now.

Aunt Bell came to the back of the house. "Joyce, you need to come on out and go home," she said.

Reluctantly, I crawled out from under the house and slipped by Aunt Bell. "Go home," she said again.

Down through Uncle Sam's cornfield and to the edge of the woods I ran, skipping with relief. As I approached the bushes that led to Grandma Smith's house, I peered through to see if I could see any signs of Roger's car. Just as I was about to step out, I saw dust rising from the driveway. It had to be him. I crouched down on my hands and knees behind a bush to be out of sight when he drove by. He pulled up and stopped. Oh no! Had he seen me in the bushes?

Fear rose up in my heart. Why was he stopping? Looking closely through the bushes, I could see dust rising from another car. Thank God!

I thought he had seen me! It was my uncle Paul, who lived past Grandma Smith's house. Roger's car was facing in my direction. My hope was that he couldn't see me through the bushes as he waited for the car to pass by. The longer he sat there, the more fearful I became. Should I crawl farther back into the woods, just in case he had seen me crouching behind the bushes? Just as I was about to crawl on my belly back into the thick undergrowth, he pulled out onto the main road. Dust from the road rose like a thick cloud as he drove past me. I crawled closer to the road, where I could see the back of Roger's car. He slowed down! What was he doing now?

I continued to peer through the thick bushes that concealed me from anyone driving up or down the road. He came to a complete stop! Was he coming back? I stood up to get a clearer view as I hid behind a big oak tree near the stream I had crossed previously. Stepping forward, I placed my foot on a flat rock in the stream. I could see clearly over the bushes between me and the back of his car. Then the car started backing up. As I turned to go back into the thick bushes, my foot slipped off the rock I was standing on. Down I went into the cold water. I bit my lip to keep from screaming. Tears filled my eyes and fear filled my heart. Had he heard the splash of the stream when I fell? I crawled out of the stream to the bank. My knees were bleeding and my clothes were all wet. I looked like a wet rat caught in a spring rain!

Now I was in real trouble. Not only was my dress ripped, but I was also wet, and my knees were all bloody from falling on the rocks. I for sure would receive a whipping I would never forget. However, that was the last thing on my mind. As I sat on the bank, trying to get my emotions under control, I quietly brushed off the dirt and blood from my knees. Suddenly I heard the car start and then stop by the bridge that led to Aunt Bell's house. It stopped for a short moment and then I heard its tires moving against the gravel road as dust once again rose from the road in a thick cloud. Scrambling to my feet, I could see clearly that the car was driving away. Cautiously, I moved closer to the road. The car seemed to be speeding up.

I gazed intensely through the bushes at the back of the car as it drove away. Nevertheless, I would not come out until the dust rising behind the car was no longer visible. As the car continued to fade into the distance, a sigh of relief came from my lips. I was still shaking with fear from the whole ordeal, and at the front of my mind was the whipping I would probably receive when I returned to Grandma Smith's house. Not only had I run away, but I had also ripped my dress, gotten all wet, and skinned my knees. I knew I had better think fast about this whole situation and find a solution for my wet clothes and bloody knees.

Slowly, I entered the road that led to Grandpa and Grandma Smith's house. Looking in all directions to make sure that no one was driving up the road and my sister Deborah wasn't sneaking around so she could go tell Grandma Smith, I ran cautiously across the road and entered the cornfield. Crouching down between the rows of corn, I made my way to the barn. It was the middle of the afternoon, and Grandpa Smith would not be coming to the barn to feed the livestock until the evening, so I would probably be safe there until my clothes dried. I found a rag in the barn that Grandpa Smith sometimes used to rub down the mules, and I cleaned the blood off my legs and knees with it. Maybe by the time my dress finally dried, Grandma Smith would have cooled down, and she would forget about giving me a whipping.

As I lay down in front of the wagon beside the corn shed in the cool green grass, the warm sun beamed down on my face, giving me a peaceful feeling. The flowers Grandma Smith had planted beside the garden filled the air with their sweet aroma. The pleasant surroundings almost made me forget what had happened just minutes before. Lying in the sun, I drifted off to sleep.

However, the peaceful sleep was soon interrupted by the voice of Deborah. Startled, I jumped to my feet.

"Leave me alone," I said.

"I'm going to tell Grandma Smith where you are," she teased.

"Please don't!" I begged. With no compassion, she ran down the road that led from the barn to Grandma Smith's house. I felt my dress. It was dry. A sigh of relief filled my heart. I was still afraid—God only knew what Deborah had told Grandma Smith. I finally mustered up enough courage to come out from behind the barn. I could see clearly that Deborah was sitting on the porch with Grandpa and Grandma Smith. I would have to pay the consequences of running away and ripping my dress, but I had to face Grandma Smith at some point. Might as well get it over with!

I was afraid to look up, so I kept my head down, looking at the ground the whole time. I walked between the rosebushes that led to the walkway. As I reached the porch, Grandma Smith spoke up. "Where you been?"

I slowly sat down in the big porch swing, holding my dress so Grandma Smith couldn't see that I had ripped it on the fence. Tears filled my eyes, and I started crying uncontrollably.

"Shut that crying up," said Grandma Smith. Afraid that at any moment she might reach out to grab my arm and drag me to the woodshed for a whipping, I sat halfway in the swing, ready to run at a moment's notice. I continued to cry. Grandma Smith told me once again to shut up my crying or she would lay a switching to my legs.

"But Grandma!" I said, "I was afraid of that strange man you called my father."

"Child, you shouldn't have run away. He wasn't going to hurt you, and if you didn't want go home with him, I would not make you go," said Grandma Smith.

"But … but Grandma, I was afraid of him," I replied.

"There was nothing for you to be afraid of, child; now go on and play," Grandma Smith said. My blue eyes became as big as saucers. I didn't want to give her a chance to change her mind, so I jumped off the big porch and ran around to the back of the house in relief, rubbing the tears from my eyes. Holding my ripped dress in one hand and breathing a sigh of thankfulness, I entered the back door to see if I could find a safety pin for the rip in my dress. I knew I must not let Grandma Smith know I was in the house, so I tiptoed to the old sewing machine that sat in the corner. There was a pin.

Holding my dress in one hand and the pin in the other, I cautiously tiptoed outside and ran to the corner of the house. Knowing I would get a whipping if Grandma Smith caught me, I remained as quiet as possible. Just when I had finished pinning my dress, Deborah came around the corner of the house to see what I was doing.

"Go away and leave me alone; I hate you!" I told Deborah. She continued to tease me until I ran to the front yard, where Grandpa and Grandma Smith were sitting on the front porch.

"Leave her alone, Deborah, or I'll give you a whipping," Grandma Smith said. I don't think Grandma Smith ever knew I fell into the stream, but she did find out I ripped my dress. However, she must have felt sorry for me, for she never punished me. I guess she felt I had been through enough pain that day, so she let me get off free and clear. Whatever the reason, I was surely glad!

Remembering that day now, I think how rejected Roger must have felt as he drove slowly down that long, dusty road out of sight. It brings sadness to my heart. Nonetheless, how was I expected to react? I had been rejected by him and my mother from the womb. They were both practically strangers in my life. Although I did get to see my mother occasionally, I had never had any kind of relationship with Roger, nor had I laid eyes on him before that day. He was a stranger in my eyes, and I didn't want to be a part of his life then or ever. Roger did not attempt to make contact with me again until I was around eleven years old.

CHAPTER 5

Lack of Emotions

One of the first things I can remember continuously hearing about in Grandpa and Grandma Smith's conversation was the Great Depression. It had created hardness in their hearts and emotions—or a lack of emotions, you might say—that affected everyone around them, including Deborah and me. They became hoarders. If you could save it, Grandma Smith had it! On one occasion, Deborah and I were playing hide-and-seek in the house. My hiding place would be under the bed, I decided. However, to my surprise, Grandma Smith had so many canned food items stored under the bed that I was unable to squeeze my skinny, long legs underneath to make it a hiding place.

I questioned Grandma Smith about all the canned food under the bed. All I remember her saying was, "Saving for hard times. You never know what will happen."

Fear of the Depression seemed to linger on their minds every day. It pressed hard on their minds and was part of their conversations. They would sit for hours, talking to whoever would listen about the hard times and how only by the grace of God they had endured and been delivered from the clutches of disaster.

Uncle Ned always said, "Grandpa Smith's bank was a fruit jar in a hole he dug in the front yard and covered up with dirt." No one really knew if that was true, but many times I found myself looking around in the front yard, trying to find any place that might be Grandpa Smith's hiding place.

Grandpa Smith always said, "You can't trust those banks! They'll take your money and leave you high and dry. Better to keep it close by, just in case one of those Depressions hits again." Because of the hardship they endured, they had acquired hard shells that prevented them from showing any emotions.

Grandpa Smith was very frugal. Memories of him rubbing his fingers over each coin for a few moments before he gave them to the cashier at the local hardware store are still fresh in my mind. Grandpa Smith always thought twice about spending what little money he had acquired by selling cows at the farmers' market. The pain of the Depression had left a deep-rooted impression of lack on their hearts and souls, to the point they seemed to be miserable about life in general.

Grandma Smith only cried a few times that I remember. In her, that same deep-rooted pain and hurt left no room for emotions or love. I have no memories of them showing any compassion or love. There was never a time that they placed us on their laps, hugged us, and said, "I love you." Love wasn't something expressed or even talked about when I was a child. It appeared it was off limits. When questions were raised, Grandma Smith always replied, "Just be happy that you have food to eat and a warm bed to sleep in. No more talking about all that stuff! It is time to go work in the field."

It seemed the answer to everything was to go work in the corn field! Deborah and I always knew when it was time to shut up and grab our garden hoes and get to work. Lingering around and asking more questions would become very painful on our backsides! Grandma Smith did not have time or tolerance to listen to what she considered two foolish little girls whose mother had left them behind, leaving her responsible for their care. Somehow, the hard-shell attitude that a generational curse of lack had brought to Grandpa and Grandma Smith's lives would go on to invade the lives of Deborah and me. Would we ever overcome the negative attitude and break the generational curse that had been spoken over our young lives?

CHAPTER 6

Gypsy Spirit

Mother was gone for long periods of time working as a caretaker for the elderly—or else just gone, with no one knowing where she was. It was as though she had a swinging door in her life. In one day, out the next. See you in six months, or maybe a year. Mother seemed to have a gypsy spirit that gripped her very soul. Wandering from place to place, she never seemed to settle down for an extended period. Her neglect of all responsibilities toward two little girls who just wanted someone to show them some kind of affection was evident from her actions.

It was as if she continually looked for love, but never found it. An expression of sadness and pain was always present on her face. Her eyes showed little or no signs of happiness, only deep hurt reflected from the depths of her soul. The relationships she searched for only seemed to lead her down a road of more rejection and pain. Nothing seemed to work out in her favor, nor did she make any decisions that would produce positive results in her life. The black hole of emptiness just sucked her in day after day, like a cancer of destruction. Each day, she appeared to roam around like a lost sheep looking for its shepherd. There was no peace for a young woman who experienced tremendous loss for so many years.

Deborah and I saw very little of Mother as we grew up. When we did, she always seemed to be more focused on herself and her problems than the hearts and lives of her daughters. She never had any time for her two girls who felt nothing but rejection. She had a life to live and places to go that didn't include us. The responsibility of raising us was placed on the shoulders of our Grandpa and Grandma Smith. Thank God for grandparents. Even if they didn't show us love, we always had the security of a warm bed and food to eat.

One day, Mother returned home with the new man in her life. I remember that Ben was very large, and he had a glass eye. Deborah and I would try to catch Ben asleep so we could look at his glass eye. We hadn't seen anything like it before, and we were two curious girls.

On one occasion Ben was asleep in the rocking chair. We tiptoed through the door as quietly as we could to look at his glass eye. Then, Mother came into the room just as we were close enough to see.

"What you girls up to?" she said.

"Nothing," we replied. We ran outside, laughing and making fun of Ben's glass eye the whole way.

We soon found out why Mother had come home. The signs were there: she was pregnant. The new man in her life appeared to love her, and they were engaged to be married—or that was the story. I have memories of Grandpa taking Ben outside to have a talk with him. I don't really know what all they discussed, but I heard Grandpa Smith tell Grandma Smith that Ben had reassured him they were getting married.

However, the marriage would not take place until much later. It was a cool May night when Mother went into labor. Because it was late at night, the only help Mother had was a country doctor who lived twenty miles away. He arrived just in time to deliver a new baby boy she would name Junior. Junior and Mother would continue to live with Grandpa and Grandma Smith. Ben would continue to visit Junior and Mother on the farm. Memories of the love I felt for Junior still linger in my mind.

He was like a doll to me. I loved touching and cuddling him. He was so soft and cute! I was not allowed to pick him up because Mother was afraid I might drop him, yet my arms longed to hold him. Finally, one day I talked Mother into letting me hold him. Her instructions were to hold Junior as I sat in the swing while she went to the kitchen for a bottle of milk.

"Don't you get up and try to walk around with him," were her instructions.

"But Mother, I want to walk him around in the warm sunlight," I said.

"You are much too young to be carrying him around by yourself. You sit right here until I get back," Mother replied.

Too young! I thought. *I will show them what a big girl I am.* Standing up, I walked off the porch. Good so far! Junior was in the warm sun and I was so happy to be holding him like a big girl. Then all of a sudden, the dog ran in front of me. Down I went on the sidewalk on top of Junior. He gave out a horrifying scream at the top of his lungs. Mother came running out of the house and grabbed Junior, who was still screaming. She turned to me as mad as a hornet and raised her hand to slap me. I pulled back as I lay on the sidewalk sobbing, with bloody knees from where the concrete had peeled off my skin.

Mother turned and said, "I will take care of you later." She ran into the house, holding Junior. Slowly regaining my strength, I pulled myself up and walked to the porch. Blood was running down my legs from the fall. No one seemed to care that I was hurt, too. Disobedience had gotten me into a ton of trouble! I knew that when Mother had Junior's situation under control, I'd be headed for the woodshed for a whipping. I was really afraid that Mother might beat me to death. Fear kept me out of the house, even when I wanted to know that Junior was okay. I decided it would be better for me to go to the stream behind the house and wash the blood off my legs and knees. Mother needed time to cool down before she gave me that whipping she had promised. Knowing that if Mother didn't cool down she would let loose on me and beat me half to death, I decided to stay out of her sight as long as I could.

Junior cried for what seemed forever. *I must have hurt him real bad,* I thought to myself. Feelings of sadness filled my heart, because I really loved Junior and I would never intentionally hurt him. Surely Mother knew that?

Darkness was falling, and I was afraid of the dark, so I finally got up enough nerve to go into the house. Grandma Smith had supper ready, but Mother couldn't leave Junior by himself.

"Something just isn't right," Mother said. As I approached the supper table, not a word was spoken. It was an eerily silent atmosphere. I assumed by their actions that everyone was upset with me, because no one asked how I was doing or tried to comfort me in any way. I wasn't very hungry, because I was still worried about Junior. I could hear him in the bedroom crying again. My greatest fear was that Junior would die. If that happened, I would surely die with him, and we would be buried side by side in a cold grave, because Mother would beat me to death for disobeying her orders.

As night continued to fall, Junior became extremely ill. He began to run a fever and started vomiting. Mother tried everything she knew to reduce his fever, but nothing seemed to help. Grandpa Smith finally had Aunt Bell call the doctor and ask him to come to the house. Yes, back then the doctors would make house calls for those who couldn't get to the office. I started praying as hard as I could, pleading with God to make Junior well. *Please, God, it was just an accident. I didn't mean to hurt him. Please make him well.* I knew in my heart that as soon as things settled down, I would be headed for the woodshed for sure. That would be okay with me just as long as Junior didn't die, I told God. *Please make him well, please.*

When the doctor arrived, he entered the bedroom where Junior lay, still sick. I peeked through the crack in the open door, still worried he would die and it would be my fault. Aunt Bell took me by the arm and pulled me away from the door, saying, "You have caused enough problems. Get over there and sit down out of the way."

After the examination, the doctor gave Junior a shot in the hip. He gave out a big loud cry, and I almost jumped out of my skin with fear. I thought the doctor was here to help Junior! Why was he crying so loudly? Had his condition become worse?

After a few minutes that seemed like an eternity to me, Junior stopped crying and drifted off to sleep. At first, it entered my mind that he might be dead. Tears filled my eyes, and my heart was pounding in my chest. Then I heard Doctor Martin say, "I think he will be fine, but you do need to bring him to the office tomorrow so I can check out his condition." Those words were music to my ears! I still don't know what was in the shot that Doctor Martin gave Junior, but I do know it relieved his pain. He stopped crying, and he didn't die! The prayer of a little country girl had been answered.

Ben, Junior's father arrived before Doctor Martin left. Grandpa Smith pulled Ben aside, and I heard Grandpa say he needed to take care of the bill for Doctor Martin's visit. Ben nodded his head, gesturing that he would take care of the bill. Ben walked Doctor Martin to the door and asked him how much the bill was. I couldn't hear the amount, but I saw Ben take some money out of his wallet and hand it to Doctor Martin. There was one thing I did know: Mother would more than likely take that same amount out of my hide with a belt to my backside!

Ben entered the bedroom where Junior and Mother were. I could hear Mother talking to Ben. However, they were talking so low I couldn't make out the conversation. Ben came out of the bedroom. Nervously, he asked Grandpa Smith about spending the night so he could take Junior to the follow-up doctor visit the next day.

No unmarried couples had ever been allowed to sleep under the same roof at my grandparents' house. Grandpa Smith looked up without saying a word and stared back at Ben with a look that said, "When hell freezes over."

Ben continued, "I'll sleep on the couch, in a chair, or in my car in the yard if you will let me stay and take Junior to the doctor."

Grandpa Smith looked up once again and, to my surprise, said, "Okay, just for tonight. Because Junior is sick, you can sleep on the couch. There will be no staying here unless you are married after tonight." Ben thanked Grandpa Smith and returned to the bedroom to check on Junior and Mother.

The next day, Ben, Mother, and Junior left for the doctor's office. Mother didn't have much to say to me before she left other than, "Get out of my way. You've caused enough problems for me, and you've hurt Junior."

I guess she was still mad, and I couldn't really blame her. Because of my disobedience, Junior had been very sick. "I didn't mean to, Mother, and I'm sorry," I tried to explain.

"Just get out of my way and out of my sight," she replied. I stepped backward out of her reach and turned to go outside. I knew if I said any more I would have double trouble when Mother returned from the doctor's office. I watched intently as they drove out of sight.

In the background, I could hear Grandma Smith calling for me to come and take the cows back to the pasture because she was through milking. In fear that Grandma Smith might scold me for the mess I had created the day before, I ran to the barn without delay. As I returned the cows to the pasture, I prayed that Junior would come back home safe and sound.

After returning from the barn, I sat in the big swing on the front porch, waiting anxiously for Ben, Mother, and Junior to pull into the driveway. Since they hadn't returned when I thought they should, I walked to the end of Grandpa Smith's driveway to see if they were coming up the road. I was really worried by this time, because they had been gone for an extended time. Suddenly, I saw dust rising in the distance. I looked more closely. It was them! I ran hard as I could back to the house and sat down in the swing, waiting to hear that Junior was going to live. They pulled up and got out of the car. I shyly approached Mother, who was carrying Junior in a blanket. I followed Mother as she stepped onto the porch. I was trying desperately to peek into the blanket to see if he was alive. Grandma Smith came out of the house and met Mother on the porch.

"Well, how is Junior?" Grandma Smith inquired.

"He's going to be okay," Mother replied. What sweet music to this little girl's ears again!

Mother seemed a little calmer since her return from the doctor. Maybe Ben had talked to her. I could only hope so! Night was about to fall, and I was still waiting for the whipping I anticipated would be coming my way. I had sat around on pins and needles all afternoon, waiting to be taken to the woodshed. Yet still not a word from Mother. Maybe I deserved it because I had disobeyed, but deep down my hope was that I would get a pass on this one! I kept waiting and waiting for the other shoe to drop, as they say, but not a word! I went to bed that night hoping and praying Mother would forgive and forget about the whipping she had promised.

The next morning we would rise early to attend the little country church about seven miles down the road. I was sitting outside on the back porch singing a song. Mother appeared behind me. I jumped off the porch in fear she would jerk me up and lay a belt to my hide. However, to my surprise, the only thing she did was to shake her finger at me and say, "Don't you ever pick Junior up again." I had escaped the lashing I had assumed I would never forget. You can believe I never picked him up again! Mother seemed relieved that Junior was okay, so she just forgot about the whole matter and moved on. Thank God she had let me pass on this one, because I knew for sure I would never have survived the switching she would have laid to my hide.

CHAPTER 7

Empty Bed

Time passed, and everything seemed to be going well. However, in the background of Mother's life, that same gypsy spirit kept raising its ugly head. She seemingly couldn't settle down in one place for an extended period. Somehow, she always seemed to be like a person on the run. Never committing to anything or anybody for any length of time became a lifestyle.

One hot summer day when we returned from working in the cornfield, we were surprised to see that Mother and Junior were missing. Grandma Smith asked me to check to see if any of their clothes were missing. Sure enough, they were gone! No one knew where they had gone. She left not a note, nor did she ever call to say where they were. It was as if she had disappeared into thin air. We assumed Mother and Junior had left with Ben, but we were not really sure. Why had they left in the middle of the day, and where were they? I looked at the empty bed where Junior had laid hours before. I truly did not understand! I was heartbroken that Junior and Mother were missing.

Tears welled up in my eyes. I retreated to the big front porch swing and cried tears of rejection. Deborah and I had been left behind yet again. Many nights I cried myself to sleep wondering why she had left us behind. Day after day, we felt unwanted and unloved. My guess is that Grandma and Grandpa Smith had more on their minds than worrying about a child's insecurities and lack of love. The day came when Mother did call and let Aunt Bell know that she was in Atlanta with Ben. Knowing where she and Junior were didn't make us hurt any less. Rejected feelings flooded my young life as I was faced with the fact that Mother seemingly had never truly loved us enough to make sure we were a part of her life.

Two years passed before Mother would show up again. We had just finished lunch and were sitting on the porch, cooling off from a morning working in the field. In the distance, we saw the dust rising high from the dirt road leading to the farm. It had not rained in weeks, making the thick brown dust even more noticeable. "Wonder who that is? Must be a stranger this time of day," Grandpa Smith said. We didn't get much traffic on our dead end road. Other than the mailman, only family traveled up and down the road early in the morning and late afternoon.

As we gazed intently at the car, we realized it was a taxi. It pulled into the driveway in front of the house. The door opened, and out stepped Mother and Junior. She didn't get a warm reception from Grandpa Smith. With a surprised look, Grandpa Smith asked, "Why are you here?"

Looking pale and tired, Mother explained that Ben had died in an accident. You could tell Grandpa Smith wasn't fully buying her story. He always said she was a good liar. Nevertheless, what was he to do? She had nowhere to go.

"Can I stay until I can find a job and a place to stay?" she asked. Grandpa Smith reluctantly agreed with the condition that as soon as she could, she needed to find a job and a place to live on her own.

"There's more to this than meets the eye. The truth will come out soon," he said. Deep down, I think Grandpa Smith knew she might be pregnant, yet again.

CHAPTER 8

Time Did Tell

Mother had become good at hiding her pregnancies. She always seemed to want the security of Grandpa and Grandma Smith's home when she was in trouble. Maybe that was the only security she could count on, because of the pain and loss she had endured throughout her life.

Grandpa Smith was right: time did tell. She could only hide it for a short period, because she was well into her sixth month when she returned home. Pregnant, lonely, and without a husband, she seemed reluctant to share any details about Ben's death. Her face was showing signs of aging, and her hair seemed grayer than when she left. Mother was quiet as the next three months went by. She didn't say much, just waited for her fourth child to be born. A few months later, she brought another baby girl into the world. However, this time it would be different. Mother had this baby at the hospital instead of Grandma and Grandpa Smith's house. Days later Mother returned home, but without our baby sister! I was confused and really didn't understand. Where was the baby? The story was that Grandpa Smith had told her he couldn't take care of any more of her children and she sure couldn't either, considering that her husband had just passed away. Mother refused to hear of such a thing. However, Aunt Bell, her sister, stepped in and had the baby girl placed for adoption.

Without Ben to help raise this child, she would be a hardship not only for Grandma and Grandpa Smith, but also for Mother. Mother reluctantly gave into the wishes of Aunt Bell. I can remember Mother crying when she came home without that baby girl. My guess is that she was sad in her own way that she had given her daughter up for adoption. However, she really didn't have much of a say in the matter. She had nowhere to live except Grandpa and Grandma Smith's house, and Grandpa Smith was not willing to take on another responsibility. Mother didn't say much about the baby girl who never came home with her in front of Deborah and me. But once I heard her talking to Grandma Smith about Aunt Bell forcing her to give the baby up for adoption. I guess Aunt Bell did what she thought was best for everyone.

Sometimes I think about that baby girl, wondering where she might be and what she looks like. Nevertheless, I guess it was best for everyone, including that new baby. At least if she was adopted, her parents would love her. She wouldn't have to experience what Deborah and I had to endure at such a young age. On occasions, I wonder if the baby sister I never knew feels rejected too, because our mother had given her up for adoption. I know in my heart that she is much better off with those who chose her as their own. They had her because they wanted her, not because they felt any obligation. That in itself was more than what Deborah and I felt each day as we faced the reality that we were a burden to Grandpa and Grandma Smith.

The truth did finally come out about Ben (my brother's father). He was dead; Mother had told the truth. Yet again, Mother was faced with loss and pain.

CHAPTER 9

Roller Coaster Ride of Rejection

Shortly after Mother returned from the hospital, she left again with Junior. She was employed as a caretaker for an elderly lady. Gone again were she and Junior. Left behind were the two little girls who would once more ride a roller coaster ride of rejection. She always seemed to favor Junior over her two young girls. It was very evident that he had a place in her heart that Deborah and I could never find or were never given.

The connection between her and Junior seemed to grow stronger and stronger. Nonetheless, Deborah's and my relationship with Mother seemed to grow father and father apart. We continued to live with Grandpa and Grandma Smith while working from sunup to sundown for our keep. Mother and Junior would come to Grandpa and Grandma Smith's on occasion to visit. However, Deborah and I were left behind with feelings of rejection. Every time I ride a roller coaster, I find myself thinking about how my life as a child was so similar to a roller coaster ride. It was as if I was moving up and down inside a dark tunnel, being jerked from side-to-side and always left with an empty feeling in the pit of my stomach at the end of each day. It never seemed to bother Mother to leave Deborah and me behind. I never saw a tear fall from her eyes or any sadness in her face when we stood on the old farm porch and waved good-bye. It appeared that the bond Mother should have with her two girls just wasn't there. I always thought I must have done something extremely bad to make her feel no connection with me. Nights and days of the roller coaster rides of rejection gave me a continuous sense of insecurity and failure that tormented me as a child.

CHAPTER 10

Nightmares

Night after night, my sleep was invaded by nightmares. The very moment I fell asleep each night, I began to dream the same dream. To this day, I really don't know why I had the same dream. Fear filled my heart each night before I went to sleep. The pain I had felt the night before in my dream was fresh on my mind, and I wasn't looking forward to dreaming that dream again.

Something to cause the dream must have happened to me when I was very small, but I could never remember the incident. While I lay in bed beside Deborah, I can recall praying quietly to God. *Please, God*, I would say under my breath, *don't let me have that nightmare tonight.* I would drift off to sleep thinking everything would be fine, only to wake up crying once again and shaking from head to toe.

Grandma Smith would ask what was wrong; when I told her, she would say, "Go back to sleep. It was only a dream." If she had known how horrified I was, she would at least have taken me in her arms and hugged me tight. However, that was not in her personality, so I was left to cry quietly in the bed with the covers over my head. For some reason, I felt I was safe when I had the blankets over my head. They gave me the security and protection I needed. Anyway, it worked at the time!

The next night, I would have the same dream again. Out of nowhere, there would appear a group of people. Together, they carried a great big balloon, which seemed to take on a life by itself. It would become larger and larger until it backed me into a corner. Once it had me lodged in the corner where I could not escape, it would begin pinching my arms, legs, and face. At times the pain seemed more than I could bear. Why was I having those dreams? In the back of my mind I was sure something bad had happened to cause them, but what? Now, I realize that someone in the family was continually picking on me and teasing me about something. Maybe someone had abused me by pinching me when I was very small, and it manifested through my dreams. However, as a small child, I could never figure out why I was so afraid at night.

On one occasion, Uncle Ned came to Grandpa and Grandma Smith's house for a visit. He was in the military and only came home a few times that I remember. He loved playing tricks and frightening people. He seemed to enjoy seeing their reactions. We never knew when he was coming for a visit. He would just show up in his big, shiny car dressed in his military uniform and shiny shoes. Uncle Ned was a handsome young man, as I recall.

One warm fall day, I was playing on the back porch and waiting for Grandma Smith to come out of the outhouse that was located down the hill from the house. (Yes, my grandparents had an outhouse. Grandpa Smith always said, "No toilet should be in the house. That thing should be located outside because it smells too bad!" Each time I think about what he said, I can't help but laugh!) This day seemed no different from any other day. I had no idea that Uncle Ned had arrived for a visit. As most children do, I was playing and talking to an imaginary friend, never realizing that Uncle Ned was standing behind me, listening and waiting for his chance to scare the living daylights out of me. Suddenly, I heard something dragging its feet behind me. Glancing over my shoulder, I saw an ugly, old man with a big, warty nose and a scary face! I froze in fear and could not move.

Without warning he said, "Boo, little girl! I've come to get you!" Screaming, I jumped to my feet and leaped off the porch that stood high off the ground, never thinking that I might break a bone. I just needed to get as far away from that ugly man as possible! I don't think my feet hit the ground more than three times before I jumped into the arms of Grandma Smith, who was just coming out of the old outhouse.

I was sobbing uncontrollably and shaking like a leaf. Grandma Smith looked up and saw Uncle Ned taking off his Halloween mask, smiling from ear to ear.

"Get down, child. It's just your Uncle Ned," she said.

"No, Grandma Smith, it's an old ugly man with a big nose," I sobbingly answered. Grandma Smith walked back up the hill, and I hid behind her every step of the way. After lingering in the backyard for a short time, I finally got enough courage to cautiously walk around the house and peek in through the screen door. There sat Uncle Ned, as handsome as ever! The ugly man was gone. However, I wasn't ready to give Uncle Ned the chance to frighten me again. I sat down on the front porch, close to the screen door, and listened as he talked with Grandma Smith.

I loved hearing Uncle Ned talk about all the places he had been and how beautiful they were. Someday, maybe I would get the chance to see all those beautiful places, too. Uncle Ned waited for Grandpa Smith to return from the barn, but time passed, and Grandpa Smith still hadn't returned. I heard Uncle Ned tell Grandma Smith he was going to the barn to find Grandpa Smith.

"I think I'll put my old ugly mask on and see if I can scare Poppy," Uncle Ned said to Grandma Smith.

"You had better be careful. Your dad doesn't like foolishness going on," replied Grandma Smith.

"I know, but it will be funny to see his reaction," said Uncle Ned.

I decided I would follow close behind to see what would happen when Uncle Ned approached Grandpa Smith. Grandpa Smith was cleaning out the horse's stables. Uncle Ned approached the barn door with caution. I could see that Grandpa Smith's back was to the door. Uncle Ned spoke in an awful, eerie voice. Grandpa Smith turned to see who it was. There in the doorway stood an old ugly man with warts and scars all over his face. Grandpa Smith paused and then said in a loud voice, "Who are you? You had better leave that barn doorway now, or you will be leaving with a pitchfork in you head." Uncle Ned knew Grandpa Smith would follow through with his words, so he took off the Halloween mask to reveal his face. Good thing Uncle Ned did, because Grandpa Smith already had the pitchfork raised and ready to release. Red-faced and mad as a hornet, Grandpa Smith turned and started cleaning the stable again.

"You best go on back to the house. I don't have time for your foolishness," Grandpa Smith said to Uncle Ned. Uncle Ned tried to talk with Grandpa Smith, but he wasn't in any mood to talk, nor was he interested in anything Uncle Ned had to say.

"Get on back to the house like I told you to," said Grandpa Smith. Uncle Ned turned with a red face, walked back to the house, and sat down on the big front porch.

"I told your dad would get mad at you," said Grandma Smith.

"Yep, I guess I should have listened to you," replied Uncle Ned. Seeing that a grown-up had been scared, just like me, made me feel a little better. However, it wouldn't help when night fell. Once again, I would be faced with bad dreams. When Grandpa Smith finally came to the house, I heard him tell Uncle Ned that he had better never play a trick like that again. I guess Uncle Ned took Grandpa Smith at his word, because I don't ever remember him scaring Grandpa Smith or me again.

However, that night my sleep would be disturbed by the big balloon pinching me in a corner, as well as the big, ugly, warty man. Even knowing it was my Uncle Ned under the mask didn't help. I woke up crying and screaming at the top of my lungs. Grandma Smith just told me to go back to sleep. Even having Deborah in the same bed didn't seem to give me much comfort or security. The nightmares would continue, and each time I would crawl as far under the covers as possible and hide my head. I guess the covers were the only security that gave comfort to that fearful little child in the middle of those dark, scary nights.

CHAPTER 11

Walking in Fear

The farm was a place I both loved and hated. When I was four years old,

 my grandpa made a special garden hoe for me so I could work in the fields. It was much shorter than a regular garden hoe. It made me feel special, because no one else on the farm had a little garden hoe like mine. If I had known back then what I know now, I would have run in the other direction when Grandpa Smith tried to place that garden hoe in my hand. Getting it meant there was no turning back from the hard work that lay before me. The work on the farm would become something I hated with a passion. My days were consumed with the dream of leaving someday and never looking back.

Everyone worked hard on that dirt farm to make a living and put food on the table. There were no exceptions; everyone who lived in Grandma and Grandpa Smith's house worked. Our days began at sunup and ended at sundown, except on Saturday and Sunday. On Saturdays, Grandpa and Grandma Smith would get Aunt Bell or Aunt Lucy to drive them to town to get a few groceries. Grandpa Smith would only allow Grandma Smith to buy those items we absolutely could not grow on the farm. Things like sugar, flour, coffee, kool-aid, and cornflakes. I never remember Grandpa Smith working on Sunday except to feed the livestock. He believed that Sunday was God's day and insisted that all who lived in his house would respect the "Lord's Day." That's what the Good Book said and he would abide by the Commandment to "Remember the Sabbath day, to keep it holy. Six days you shall labor do all your work, but the seventh day is the Sabbath of the Lord your God" (Exodus 20: 8–10, NKJV).

Playing on Sundays was also generally forbidden for the children who lived in his house. After church on Sundays, our recreation consisted of sitting in the swing on the big farmhouse porch, listening to the grown-ups talk about the "good ole days" before the Depression and swatting flies with a fly swatter. Grandma Smith did a lot of her cooking on Saturday for Sunday dinner, and we ate leftovers for supper on Sundays. Sunday afternoons were lazy days on the farm. The majority of the time I would fall asleep in the swing on the front porch listening to the grown ups talking, cows mooing, and the voices of crickets, katydids, and tree frogs. I never seemed to be able to sleep for very long before being awakened by something crawling on my face, usually flies from the barn. Nevertheless, as I opened my sleepy eyes, Grandpa and Grandma Smith would always still be talking about the "good ole days" and how the younger generations were going to hell in a hand basket because they would not listen to their parents. Sounds a lot like what we say today about this younger generation! Not much fun, but we knew better than to break Grandpa Smith's rules without asking his permission. He had put the fear of God in our young hearts, and we stood up and listened when he spoke.

Laughter wasn't something I was accustomed to. I could probably count on one hand the times I saw Grandpa and Grandma Smith laugh. I do remember once seeing Grandpa Smith dance on the old hearth in front of the fireplace. We didn't have a TV, but we did have a radio. Grandpa Smith would listen to the *Grand Ole Opry* every Saturday night. On one occasion, he got up and clogged with the music. That was about the extent of the laughter we experienced. I don't really know where he learned to clog, but I guess maybe he had gone to a few barn-dancing parties when he was a teenage boy. There was one thing for certain: Grandpa Smith would never let the preacher at our country church know he had been dancing. We were taught by the church that a praying knee and a dancing foot didn't belong on the same leg. It was one of those things that would send you straight to hell, so you better not be caught doing it. Isn't it funny how we make a religion out of a saying that has been handed down from generation to generation?

Deborah and I had little to no time to laugh and have fun. There was work to be done: crops to be planted, cows to milk, and livestock to feed. That was what Grandpa and Grandma Smith lived for, and if you lived in their house that would be your life, too. Working was the force that controlled every minute of Grandpa and Grandma Smith's lives. They had no time to laugh or play. I often wondered how they could spend so much time in the field with the hot sun beating down on their heads day after day.

Their drive to work the farm in extreme heat gave Deborah and me no excuses. We were only allowed to stop working when Grandpa Smith gave us his permission. If we were caught goofing off, we stood the chance of getting our legs whipped with the reins that guided the mules. He had no time for foolishness, and goofing off would not be tolerated.

We would cultivate row after row of corn. Memories of hard days of work still are fresh in my mind. Grandpa Smith put the fear of God in our young hearts about cutting down his corn by mistake. I was so fearful that whenever I weeded around the rows, I would dig down deep into the dirt and pile lots of dirt around the corn stalks to prevent them from falling over.

I developed a fear of men partially because my Grandpa Smith was very strict and always demanded we obey, regardless of the circumstances. We were never given the chance to explain our side of anything. In Grandpa and Grandma Smith's eyes, we did not have a side to explain. We were to do everything in their way and never talk back. If we had, they would probably have slapped our eyes out through the back side of our head, so we would be looking at where we had been instead of where we were going! All Grandpa Smith had to do was speak, and I knew I had better line up with what he said. You might say he put the fear of God in me, and I stood up and listened when he called my name!

Many days I stood in the cornfield and prayed for God to send either a cloud to cover my head from the sun, or rain so we could go into the house and rest. However, if it did rain, we were only allowed to sit on the porch swing and watch it rain. Grandma Smith didn't allow us to sit on our beds after they were made up. That was a rule you had better not get caught breaking, or you would end up in the woodshed with a limb across your legs. "Only lazy people lie on the bed in the middle of the day," she would say. Anyway, she didn't like our feet on her nice clean bedspreads. If she caught you with your feet anywhere close to the bedspread, you were in a heap of trouble. So we remained on the front porch.

I can remember smelling those fresh summer rains as we sat quietly, watching them pound against the dusty driveway that led to Grandpa and Grandma Smith's house. The ground seemed to soak up the rain like a sponge as the trees, leaves, flowers, and windswept grass danced with joy. The quiet moments were like the voice of God's nature orchestrating its music to bring us a refreshing, peaceful day. On a few occasions, I fell asleep while it was raining and woke up to a ray of warm sunshine peeking through the puffy white clouds and shining on my face. If the sun began to shine again and it didn't rain too hard, we would return to the field and work until almost dark. But on many days, God answered a child's prayer, and it rained so hard it was impossible to return to the field. Those were the days I liked most. Even in those early days, God was answering the prayers of a young child who had no idea about a loving Father. She had never experienced the arms of an earthly loving father around her in any form. So to call God her Father was strange to that country girl.

CHAPTER 12

Ruled with a Strong Disciplinary Hand

Grandpa and Grandma Smith had worked hard all their lives, and the results of that work showed in deep wrinkles in both their faces. Working hard in the sun had taken a toll on them, yet they always seemed to have the strength to do a little more each day to make ends meet. After a day in the hot sun, we all headed for the barn. My job was to get the cows, bring them to the barn for milking, and then return them to the pasture. I hated that job, because it meant most of the time I would have to stay out after dark. On many occasions, I would have to walk long distances to another pasture to get the cows and return them to our barn. When it was dark, fear would grip my very soul! The vision of something jumping out and attacking me from the dark areas in the forest would almost freeze me in my tracks. Nonetheless, fear of Grandpa Smith's taking a belt to my hide kept me moving those cows into the pasture as swiftly as I could. I would sing, talk loud, and run like a race horse so I could quickly get back to the barn and in the presence of Grandpa Smith, who was still feeding the mules.

After all the chores were completed, we would return to the house to eat our supper. Yes, we called it supper. Grandma Smith would leave the barnyard first after milking the cows and have supper all ready on the old wood stove that sat in the corner of the kitchen. While supper was cooking, she strained the milk and prepared it for the churn. She made the best homemade butter and buttermilk you could ever desire! The aroma of Grandma Smith's fried potatoes would make my mouth water. You could hear them crackling and popping against the lid that covered the old iron skillet on that wood-burning stove. She fried them brown and crisp in the lard she made from pigs Grandpa Smith killed in the fall. I would stand and watch her flip and toss them in the pan, making sure they didn't burn or stick. The aroma filled the air, making me anxious to get to the table and dig in. I can smell those fried potatoes right now. We had fried potatoes, pinto beans, and cornbread most nights, but I never remember getting tired of going to the table and eating them over and over. In their house you had better not complain about what Grandma Smith placed on the table. It would be bad news for you if you did! Luckily, everything Grandma Smith prepared tasted good to me. Man, I miss her fried potatoes. I wonder sometimes if Grandma Smith is preparing God Himself a pan of her fried potatoes in Heaven.

Once the table was prepared with food, we would be called to come and eat. When you were called, you had better show up at the table quickly or suffer the consequences of Grandpa Smith's wrath. His rule was that no one would sit down at the table after he had started eating. As children, we were not allowed to speak a word while eating at the table unless we were asking for Grandpa Smith to spoon out some food from the bowl onto our plates. Grandpa Smith believed children were to be seen and not heard.

We always had to say "thank you" before we received a spoonful of potatoes or cornbread or whatever else Grandma Smith had prepared. It was disrespectful in the eyes of Grandpa Smith not to say "thank you," and we would pay a dear price if we made that mistake. Our choices were to leave the table, even if we were still hungry, or to be slapped across the face with Grandpa Smith's big, rough hand. There was an occasion when Deborah came to the table with hair curlers in her hair. That was a big mistake! Grandpa Smith told her to get up and leave the table. "You are not sitting at this table with those things in your hair," he said.

Grandpa Smith expected respect and obedience, and that is what he got from Deborah and me. No back talk was allowed in their house. You did as they said or you would be looking at the end of a belt, and you might be missing a few teeth the next time you looked in the mirror. Grandpa Smith ruled with a strong disciplinary hand and a big brown belt that I grew to respect and fear. On many occasions, that big brown belt came down from its hook on the back of the bedroom door. I tried very hard to stay in line with what I was told, because I knew what the end result would be if I didn't. Grandpa Smith had become a hard man through the years because of the hardship he had endured. That hardship would invade the lives of Deborah and me. Childhood was riddled with fear and rejection for two young children who were confused the majority of the time about their situation.

CHAPTER 13

Hill of Beans

Negative words fell on my ears as a young child. I never realized how powerful words could be until I began to study Proverbs 18:12, "Death and life are in the power of the tongue …" I realized for the first time how a person could speak into a child's life and the fruits of those words could affect the child for many years.

Many days I heard these words from Grandma Smith's lips: "You  are just like your mother, and you, too, will never amount to a hill of beans." I used to wonder what a hill of beans had to do with how I would turn out. But I knew it was not good and that my Grandma Smith really didn't think I was worth spending energy on. Deborah and I worked like horses on the farm to earn our keep. It seemed that no matter how hard we tried, we always fell short of what we should have done. If we brought the wood in for the cook stove, we stacked it the wrong way. If we hoed the corn, we didn't get all the weeds out of it. If we carried the slop to feed the pigs, we spilled too much of it before we reached the pig pen. The list went on and on!

On one occasion, the cows broke through the fence and crossed over into the mountains. It took me a long time to find them and head them back to the barn to milk. Grandpa and Grandma Smith were waiting at the gate with a disgusted look on their faces. What had I done wrong? I wondered. As I approached the barn gate, the negative words began.

"Where have you been? Why has it taken so long? You've been lagging around and made us late milking the cows," were the words from Grandpa and Grandma Smith's lips. It did no good to try to explain my side of the story. They were not interested in excuses from a stupid little girl who, in their opinion, didn't have enough sense to get in out of the rain. Besides they had said I wouldn't amount to a hill of beans in their eyes. I began to cry because I really didn't know what I had done wrong. It was not my fault the cows had broken through the fence and gone deep into the mountain terrain looking for grass to eat. You had better believe that I looked as hard and fast as I could to get out of those mountains before dark, because I was afraid of the dark! I for sure didn't want to be up there with those black panthers that wandered down to the farm on many occasions.

Grandma Smith had little patience with my crying because she needed to get the cows milked so she could prepare supper. She said, "Go sit down out of my way while I milk the cows." My mistake was standing in the doorway much too long crying. To my surprise, as Grandma Smith milked, she turned and aimed the udder in my direction, spraying my face with milk. "Now, get on out of here like I told you to," she said.

Running to the wagon under the shed, I continued to cry. After about thirty minutes, I heard Grandma Smith yelling for me to stop that crying and get the cows back to the pasture. I slowly walked by her as she swatted at me with a limb she had in her hand. "Get it done now and get back to the house in time for supper or you will get a whipping," she said. We never seemed to get anything done fast or good enough for Grandpa and Grandma Smith. A little confused as to why Grandma Smith was so mad at me, I ran as hard as I could to make sure I was not late for supper.

When I entered the house, I could hear Grandma and Grandpa Smith talking about how they couldn't depend on me to do anything right. The negative words penetrated my heart like a knife. I was really confused about the whole situation and what had just taken place. My heart was broken, but I had better not show it, or I would for sure get that whipping she had promised me at the barn. Grandma Smith looked up from the milk she was straining as I entered the kitchen shyly. "Get out of the way. All I need is you under my feet," she snapped. I stepped backward. She continued pouring milk into the churn to make buttermilk and homemade butter. I loved Grandma's homemade butter on a hot biscuit with jelly. No one makes homemade biscuits with butter and jelly like my Grandma Smith did when she was alive. They were so delicious they would melt in your mouth.

"Can I churn the milk, Grandma Smith?" I said.

"No. You'll only make a mess, and I don't have time to clean up a mess. Go to the front porch and sit down with your grandpa until I get supper ready," she replied. With tear-filled eyes, I turned to go to the front porch. I didn't dare let her see me crying. As I sat down in the big front porch swing, I said not a word. Grandpa Smith was a quiet man who had little to say most of the time—unless we were out of line. Then bar the door, Katie, because it was on. Anyway, in his eyes I didn't have anything to say that he was interested in hearing. So I sat quietly, waiting to be called for supper.

Dark was approaching, and Deborah and I would have to finish supper, clean the dishes, and bathe in the wash pan before going to bed. Grandpa Smith didn't like for us to turn the lights on in the house. I often wondered why he had the house wired with electric light. We knew we had better work fast and get everything done before dark, or his big brown belt would appear. Grandpa had little tolerance or time for two foolish little rejected girls who were another responsibility he hadn't asked for and who, most of the time, we felt he didn't want. However, he and Grandma Smith did take on the responsibility of caring for us when no one else would. For that, we needed to be thankful. Still, as I think about how we had negative words spoke over us day after day, I really wonder how we ever made it through to become responsible adults.

CHAPTER 14

Rhinestone Belt

Our grandparents lived in a two-bedroom house; however, Deborah and I were never allowed to have a room to ourselves. There were two beds in Grandpa and Grandma Smith's room, and that was where we slept. We were a little confused as to why we were never allowed to sleep in the empty room when no one was in town, but that was the rule, and we knew better than to question their decisions.

One night Deborah and I had gone to bed, but not yet fallen asleep. Shortly after Grandpa and Grandma Smith came in and went to bed, Deborah and I started giggling and poking at each other. Grandpa Smith rose up in the bed and said, "Girls, you had better stop that giggling and go to sleep. I have extra work to do tomorrow and I need my sleep."

Try as hard as we could, we couldn't contain the giggling. Grandpa Smith once again said, "Girls, I'll lay a belt to your hide if you don't shut up and go to sleep." We put our heads under the covers, and I put the blanket in my mouth to try to stop; however, we still were giggling. While under the covers, we were startled to hear Grandpa Smith's feet hit the floor. Oh no! We were in trouble now! The big, wide leather belt with green, red, yellow, and clear rhinestones came off the back of the door. He pulled the covers back and began to hit us on the legs and back with that big rhinestone belt. We began to scream and cry from the pain of the rhinestones hitting our flesh. Each blow of the belt seemed to rip the flesh

44

and leave big red marks in the shape of rhinestones on our legs and backs. I still remember how painful it was. It was at that point that Grandma Smith stepped in and said, "That's enough, Henry." Sobbing in pain from the whipping, we snuggled together in bed to comfort each other as much as possible.

Grandpa Smith turned and said, "Girls, shut that crying up! You're just like your mommy. You won't amount to anything." Deborah and I were sobbing hard, but we were trying to stop. We knew that Grandpa Smith would get the big belt down again if we didn't, and we were already in enough pain from the first whipping. My chest was hurting so badly from trying to stop crying that it felt like a ton of bricks lying on my chest. Still, I knew I had better get it under control, and fast! Feeling the pain of the whipping and hearing the words of rejection, I finally fell asleep, crying and holding my chest . We carried evidence of that rhinestone whipping for days! There were blue marks all over our legs and backs.

"Just a reminder," Grandpa Smith would say, "That you need to mind when I tell you to!" You had better believe Deborah and I never giggled in bed again. Fear of that rhinestone belt had made a burning impression on our minds for life.

The next morning would be more of the same for Deborah and me. Not a kind word of encouragement for two little girls who lived a life of being told we would not amount to anything. We were just like our Mother, they always said. She was nothing in Grandpa Smith's eyes, and so were we. I have said many times since then, "If Grandpa and Grandma Smith could only see me now!"

CHAPTER 15

Sour Grapes

At the early age of five, I had such a desire to go to school that Grandma Smith placed me on the big yellow school bus with Deborah at the beginning of the year and told her to place me in first grade. I was so excited to finally ride the big yellow bus my sister had been riding for several years. It was my "coming out day" to school, and I knew nothing could hold me back. World, here I come! The school was about twenty miles from our farm, so we had to get up really early to catch the big yellow school bus. It was fall, and the leaves were bright. The air had a chill in it from the frost that lay heavy on the grass. Nevertheless, nothing could put a damper on the excitement that filled my heart and soul. School was a new adventure of discovery for a five-year-old who couldn't wait to see what the world had waiting for her! I looked out the window of the school bus as we passed many cars, trucks, and buses. It was a big world to the eyes of a little blue eyed five-year-old and I couldn't wait to greet it.

The bus pulled up to the big school. We were greeted by some of the teachers and Mr. White, the principal. Deborah escorted me to the primary building, and I took in all I could as we walked down the halls. As we entered the door, the first-grade teacher asked me my name. I said, "Joyce." She looked at her attendance roll and said, "I do not have you on my register, but come on in and we will work it out later."

I sat down in what seemed to me like the biggest desk in the world.

46

I was a little afraid, but I was happy to be there, and I didn't care how big it was. My dream of entering school had become reality. As the day progressed, my teacher consulted with Mr. White. They called me to the teacher's big desk in front of the blackboard. As I slowly rose to my feet and went forward, I felt a little fear rising up in my heart; I was unsure what they were going to do or say. Mr. White explained to me that I was two weeks to young to enter school. At that time, the cutoff day was the last day of September. I would not be six years old until October.

My heart sank as I heard these words come out of his mouth. I would not be able to return to school until the next fall, because I had missed the cutoff date. With tear-filled eyes and a red face, I returned to my desk feeling rejected once again. I couldn't believe they were sending me home for another year because I was two weeks too young. All I saw was that yet another male had rejected me. It didn't matter what the circumstances were. To a five-year-old going on six, it was rejection that was crushing my very spirit. I left the school disheartened and downcast. The ride home seemed much longer than the ride to school had been that morning, when I was so excited.

I ran all the way home with tear-filled eyes to tell Grandma Smith that I couldn't go back to school until next year because I had missed the cutoff day by two weeks. Grandma Smith had little time to console a five-year-old whose heart was broken. She looked down at me and said, "Go get the cows in, so I can milk before dark."

"But, Grandma Smith, you don't understand. I can't ride the big yellow bus and go to school," I said.

She looked down again and said, "Go to the field and get the cows in right now. It will be dark soon."

I walked slowly away, disappointed that she was more interested in milking cows than in the broken heart of a little girl whose dreams of attending school had just been shattered. When I walked slower than she liked, she yelled out, "Run, don't walk, and get the cows, or I will take a switch to your legs." I ran as hard as I could with tears in my eyes. I hated the cows, and I hated my Grandma Smith, because she just didn't understand the rejection I was feeling.

That long year seemed to be an eternity, but finally fall came again, and this time the school could not send me home again. I was almost seven by the time I entered the first grade. I was always the oldest one in the class. Everyone thought I had failed a grade in school because of my age. It made me feel a little rejected by my classmates, because they were always asking why I was a year older than them. But I was excited to be in school, so I just ignored their questions about my age.

Our class was close to the lunchroom, and we could smell the cakes, cookies, and hot meals the lunchroom ladies prepared. They smelled so good. However, there was no money for us to buy lunch. Grandma Smith would pack two jelly biscuits in a big brown bag for me to take to school. I was so embarrassed to be the only one in the room with two jelly biscuits in a big brown grocery bag. My classmates had their hot plates of food with cookies and cake for lunch, while I just had two jelly biscuits. How humiliating! I felt as if I would die if anyone asked me what I had for lunch. I would almost place my whole head in the big brown bag to keep my classmates from seeing what I was eating.

One day, my worst fears became a reality. A classmate who sat beside me asked what I had for lunch. Oh no! What would I say? I pretended I didn't hear him.

"Joyce, what you got in the brown paper bag you keep sticking your head in?" he said again. Slowly, I pulled out my golden brown biscuits filled with Grandma's strawberry jelly.

"My, that looks good! I'll trade you my piece of cake for that jelly biscuit," he said. What? He wanted my jelly biscuit? What I didn't know was that those city kids wanted what I had: good old country cooking. Grandma Smith could make some tasty biscuits. So guess what? He got my biscuit, and I got his cake! We didn't get much cake at Grandma Smith's house, so that sounded good to this country girl. I couldn't wait to get home that day and tell Grandma Smith about trading one of her jelly biscuits for a piece of cake. After that day, I wasn't embarrassed about having jelly biscuits for lunch. More than once I traded a jelly biscuit for something on one of those city kids' plates. However, they always had to ask me to trade, because I was too shy to ask them.

Because I was shy, I didn't make friends easily. Most of the kids in my room didn't socialize with me except when they wanted my jelly biscuits. I was a poor kid from a dirty farm, so there was no way I would ever be the teacher's pet. I couldn't bring her gifts, nor could Grandpa and Grandma Smith come to the Parent Teacher Association meetings. I was the outcast in Ms. Walker's eyes, and she never bothered with helping me try to succeed in school. I never had paper or a pencil, because Grandpa and Grandma Smith didn't have the funds to buy them. Ms. Walker made sure that everyone in the class knew I came to school without supplies. My face would feel as hot and red as fire when she called out my name simply because I asked someone else for a piece of paper and a pencil. She would say things that belittled me in front of my classmates. I was so humiliated at the young age of six by Ms. Walker that I became fearful and hated all teachers.

On one occasion I was told that if I didn't bring a number two pencil to school the next day for a test, I would get a zero. I was devastated. What would I tell Grandma Smith? With little to no money for extras, I was sure to receive a zero. When I arrived at the farm after school, I ran to tell Grandma Smith what the teacher said. She said she would try to find one by morning. I was so afraid and felt anxious, because she kept saying, "I will do it later." "Later" had always led to me having to show up without the supplies I needed. However, I knew I had said enough. If I persisted, Grandma Smith would become angry and give me a whipping, so I let it go, hoping she would follow through. First thing next morning, I hit Grandma Smith up about the pencil.

"Grandma, did you find me a number two pencil for school today?" I said. She said no. My blood felt like it drained to my feet. What was I to do?

Grandma Smith told me to go on to school. Fear struck my heart like an arrow. How could I face that mean Ms. Walker without a number two pencil? I left the house crying uncontrollably.

"Get on out of here and go to school," Grandma Smith said. As I walked to the bus stop, tears continued to flow down my cheeks like a stream. I was late, and the bus was waiting for me. The steps into the bus seemed to be the longest ones I had ever climbed in my life—much longer than the day before. As I reached the top step, I heard Grandma Smith calling out to the bus driver to wait. She ran to the bus and placed in my hand a yellow number two pencil! Joy flooded my heart and soul. I would not be humiliated by Ms. Walker in front of my classmates today. I held that number two pencil in my hand tight as a precious diamond.

The big yellow school bus pulled in front of the schoolhouse. When the bus driver opened the door, I was one of the first off. I could hardly contain my excitement. I entered the classroom. Ms. Walker peered over her glasses. With a disgusted look, she asked, "Do you have a number two pencil, Joyce?"

With a great big smile, I answered, "Yes!" She seemed a little disappointed. With a smug look on her face, she said, "Go sit down."

Thank God Grandma Smith had found a pencil for me! God only knows what Ms. Walker would have done if I had shown up without it. I am sure I would have been the recipient of some harsh words or a spanking in addition to a grade of zero. Luckily, I didn't have to find out what else I would have had to endure at the hands of Ms. Walker, who seemed to take pleasure in humiliating me in front of my classmates. My hope was that one day I could hold my head up and not be ashamed of the fact that I did not have the school supplies to complete my homework or study in class. The first grade was a painful year, and I couldn't wait for it to end. School, which had started out as something so desirable, became a torment.

Somehow, I made it through the first grade. Unfortunately, that same rejected feeling lingered throughout all my school years. I always expected the worst from all my teachers, even the good ones. The deep scars of the first grade would prevent me from trusting any of them. Why did Ms. Walker have such a vendetta against me? Singling me out for my poverty, difficulty in comprehending, and inability to bring school supplies was an everyday occurrence in front of my classmates. Why on earth would anyone be so malicious in their actions toward a six-year-old?

My school years would continue to be filled with those rejected feelings from my bad experiences with Ms. Walker. My feeling of never being good enough for her ran over into my relationships with my classmates. When I was growing up, schoolteachers were like pastors, high on a pedestal in the eyes of most people. Whatever they said was taken as the truth. So nobody was interested to hear what I had to say about the situation at school. I was just a little farm girl who struggled to be accepted by those around her.

On one occasion, Grandma told my sister to help me with my homework. School was not high on the priority list of Grandpa and Grandma Smith. They had been required to work on their parents' farms instead of attending school. Grandpa Smith could read and write somewhat, but not enough to help me with my schoolwork. Grandma Smith couldn't read at all and could only sign her name, so I couldn't count on her. I would cry and beg for help, so finally Grandma Smith told Deborah to sit down and help me. I wasn't Deborah's favorite person, because I was a thorn in her side. She surely didn't want to help her little sister in any form. The only reason she agreed to help was that Grandma Smith most likely would have taken her to the woodshed if she had said no.

She sat down beside me. Rapidly, she started explaining my homework to me.

"Please, Deborah, slow down. I cannot understand what you are saying," I said. Deborah became irritated when I did not catch on as fast as she wanted me to.

"You are stupid, and I don't have time to mess with you," she said. Then ,suddenly, she stabbed me in the finger with her pencil. I gave out a great yell.

"Deborah stabbed my finger with her pencil, Grandma Smith!"

Grandma Smith came running to see what was wrong. Deborah lifted her pencil from my finger to reveal where it was bleeding. The lead had broken off in my finger. Grandma Smith gave her a switching that she wouldn't soon forget. To this day, I still have lead in my finger!

Deborah refused to help me again because of the switching she had received. That meant I was on my own. I tried as hard as I could, but my best wasn't always enough. Struggling would become a lifestyle that would follow me into my adulthood. I dared not tell Grandma Smith that my sister wasn't helping me, because she would make my life a living hell. Rejection from Deborah was another issue I would have to deal with as young child. I never really felt secure in my own skin because of the rejection and verbal abuse I received from family members. Those negative words probably had a lot to do with my low self-esteem and the difficulty that seemed to shadow over my life year after year.

Nevertheless, the struggles I endured in school would be a stepping-stone to helping other disadvantaged children. as an adult, I organized a charity called Operation Hand Up™ that has placed over five thousand supply-filled book bags into the hands of disadvantaged children who otherwise would have gone to school without school supplies. My daughter Renee grew up to be a first-rate schoolteacher. Her work gave me the opportunity to volunteer in her class to help children who needed a little extra help, just like I did. Yesterday's sour grapes became today's sweet success. I took yesterday's struggles and used them to help disadvantaged children see a brighter tomorrow.

CHAPTER 16

Christmas Morning Heartbreak

Christmas Day was Grandpa Smith's birthday. All my aunts and uncles always gave him something special for his birthday. For a few years, all the family members who lived close by would meet at Grandpa and Grandma Smith's house for a dinner. However, that stopped after a while. Uncle Ned and Uncle Tom would occasionally come to Grandpa and Grandma Smith's for Christmas. Deborah and I watched with anticipation for them to come because we knew we would receive something from Santa. It would probably be something very small, but that didn't matter to us as long as it was a gift from Santa.

Close to the day they would arrive for Christmas, Grandpa Smith would go out into the field to cut down a cedar tree at Grandma Smith's request. It was only when company was coming that Grandma Smith put up a Christmas tree. Grandpa Smith was hesitant because he said it was a fire hazard. "Can't afford for the house to burn down," he'd tell Grandma Smith. Grandma Smith had a mind of her own, so she would put it up anyway, and it brought joy to Deborah and me. I will never forget stringing the great big red, blue, green, and yellow lights all around the tree. We knew the whole time we were stringing them that Grandpa Smith would forbid us to plug them in. Didn't matter to us—it was exciting anyway!

Deborah and I would make chains with green paper we received from the local church. Grandma Smith would go to the corncrib and get a few ears of popcorn she had grown in the summer. She would hold it over the open fireplace in a pan and shake it like crazy so it wouldn't burn before it popped. It smelled so good that we wanted to eat some, but it was for decorating the tree, and that was more important to us than eating it. Grandma Smith would give Deborah and me a needle and thread to string each white, puffy grain into a long string bursting with beauty. We would string enough to wrap around the tree many times. We only had a few store bought ornaments, and we could not touch them because Grandma Smith was afraid we might break them.

"No money to replace them, so it's best that I hang these on the tree," she said. Deborah and I knew when we saw the tree going up that one of our uncles would be bringing a small present for us. We never received much for Christmas otherwise, except an orange and a stick of peppermint candy in an old stocking.

The Christmas tree lights were my favorite thing. How I longed to plug them in so I could see their many colors! Yet, day after day, the tree would sit there lifeless. I really never understood why Grandma bothered to put them on, knowing that Grandpa Smith didn't like for them to be plugged in. The first time I saw them plugged in; they were so beautiful that I could hardly contain my excitement. However, Grandma Smith unplugged them quickly before Grandpa Smith saw them and became angry. He was always concerned that the tree would catch on fire and burn the house down. I guess that was a good reason, but my heart ached to see them burn bright.

One day, when everyone was outside on the porch, I decided to plug them in for a few seconds. That was a mistake I will never forget. Just before I unplugged them, I was shocked to see Grandma Smith open the front door and walked into the room. My big blue eyes were big as saucers when I saw her. I almost pushed the tree over trying to get the lights unplugged.

"Child, what are you doing? Go right now and break me a switch. You are going to get a little hickory tea," Grandma Smith said. I knew hickory tea meant my legs would be stinging like a bee. I was in trouble now! Nevertheless it was worth what I had to endure to see the radiant lights come alive.

Grandpa and Grandma Smith always found a way for us to go to the little country church for the Christmas play on Christmas Eve. Deborah and I looked forward to the event, because we would receive the gift of a small brown paper bag filled with oranges, nuts, and candy. We knew that would probably be all we would receive, and we had better make the best of it. I tried to make sure I was at the front of the line, because in the past they had run out of goodie bags, leaving me empty-handed.

After the Christmas play, we would return home. It was at the tender age of seven that I experienced one of the most heartbreaking moments in my life on Christmas morning. On our return from church, Grandma Smith told Deborah and me to go to bed before Santa came and caught us up.

"He will keep on going if he comes by and you are still up," she said. Even when we didn't get anything but a stick of peppermint candy and an orange that had probably come from Grandpa and Grandma Smith's own goodie bag from the church, it was still exciting! Deborah and I rummaged through the old closet next to the fireplace looking for the old heavy stockings Grandma Smith wore to church on Sunday. We finally found two that would work. Holding them up carefully, we looked to make sure they would hold the oranges without them falling through a hole. Deborah and I placed them on two rusty nails that were already nailed above the fireplace. We were two excited little girls!

Grandma Smith said once again, "You had better hurry, because I think I hear Santa's reindeer on the roof." Deborah and I decided we had better follow Grandma Smith's instruction before Santa saw we were up! We jumped into bed, and I can remember squeezing my eyes real tight, trying to make myself go to sleep. Finally I must have fallen asleep, because the next thing I remember was the aroma of bacon cooking in the air. Man, it smelled good. I reached over and shook Deborah.

"Get up! It's time to see what Santa brought us last night," I said. She rubbed her eyes and rose up in the bed.

"Let's go see what Santa left," she said. Our feet hit the floor at the

same time. As we ran around the door, we could hear the fire crackling in the big fireplace that was used to heat the house. We ran over to Grandma's old stockings hanging on the rusty nails above the fireplace. Then we stopped in surprise. There hung Grandma Smith's old stockings as flat as pancakes on those old rusty nails, with no sign that Santa had been by our house. Deborah and I couldn't believe our eyes.

"Did Santa forget where we live?" I asked Grandpa Smith, who had a chair pulled up close to the open fire.

"No," said Grandpa. "You were not good all year. Santa doesn't deliver anything to those children who have misbehaved. When he came by, he looked down and said you would get nothing this year because you have been bad girls." Rejected, crying, sad, and confused, Deborah and I sat down on the floor in front of the crackling fire with tear-filled eyes.

I looked up at Grandpa Smith and said, "Grandpa Smith, I don't understand. Deborah and I couldn't have been that bad, could we?"

Grandpa Smith replied, "I guess you were, because you didn't get anything, did you? I'm surprised," he continued, "that Santa didn't leave you a stocking full of hickory switches because you were so bad all year. Bad girls don't receive anything from Santa."

That was the most miserable Christmas morning for two little girls who felt rejection in their hearts from Santa. "He is a mean man, and I don't like him anymore," I told Grandma Smith. That was the day Deborah and I stopped believing in Santa. Tearful and rejected by what I thought was another male in my life, I sat in the floor and cried. I guess it was a good way for Grandpa and Grandma Smith to stop even placing oranges and peppermint candy canes in our stockings. I don't remember receiving anything else on Christmas morning after that, except when my uncles occasionally came for a visit.

CHAPTER 17

Wild Bike Ride

Later in the afternoon on that Christmas Day, Aunt Bell and my cousins came over to visit Grandpa Smith for his birthday. They rode their shiny red bikes that Santa had brought them for Christmas. Deborah and I were so jealous! Why had Santa delivered shiny red bikes to them, while we had received nothing? Aunt Bell had five children, and they all had received new bikes. That Santa was mean in my eyes. Our cousins continued to ride their bikes around and around in Grandpa and Grandma Smith's driveway. It looked like it was so much fun!

Try as we might, we could not talk them into letting us ride their bikes. They teased Deborah and me about not getting anything from Santa because we were bad little girls. Finally Aunt Bell came to the door and told them to take us for a ride. My place would be on the handlebars of Cousin Martha, because she didn't trust me to ride without crashing her bike. Cousin Martha started going faster and faster down the road. I was screaming at the top of my lungs with fear, because I had never been on a bike before. Suddenly, we ran over a big hole in the road.

The bike became airborne, and we were thrown up into the air. Down we came on the hard, rocky road. Cousin Martha fell on top of me, knocking the wind out of me. I couldn't breathe, and my chest and lungs felt as if they had collapsed. Cousin Martha got up and started screaming because a spoke in the wheel had broken. I was still lying on the ground bloody and breathless, and the only thing she could think about was her bike! I still couldn't talk. At last, Cousin Martha realized I was having difficulty breathing. She pulled me to my feet and began to hit me on the back, trying desperately to get me to take in air. Finally, I was able to breathe again. However, as soon as she realized I was all right, she became furious again about her broken spoke—even though she was the one driving, not me.

Both of us finally collected ourselves and headed back to Grandma Smith's house. I was bleeding all over from our hard fall on the gravel road. Small pieces of gravel were sticking out of the skin on my knees. Blood was streaming down my legs, and I had a cut on my head where Cousin Martha had fallen on me. I was a mess, but I had cushioned her fall and kept her from being hurt .You would have thought she would have appreciated that, at least!

The day had begun on a bad note for me, and now I was all cut up, Cousin Martha was mad at me, and I would for sure get a whipping. Cousin Martha ran ahead of me so she could tell Grandma Smith and Aunt Bell that I had broken her bike. She wanted to tell her side of the story first, because she was afraid Aunt Bell might give her a whipping for driving the bike too fast. Limping back home behind her, rejected and crying, I could see Grandma Smith and Aunt Bell standing on the big old farmhouse porch. Aunt Bell wanted to know why I was on the handlebars of the bike. I tried to tell her that Cousin Martha had made me sit there, but she would not listen, because she thought her children were all angels. After all, Deborah and I were the children of the black sheep of the family, and that was enough reason to think I was the one lying. Grandma Smith didn't say much, other than that I should not have been on the handlebars in the first place. That wasn't much comfort for a little rejected girl who was bleeding from head to toe!

I have never gotten on a bike since. I always say that when I get to Heaven, God will have a special gold bike just for me, and He will personally teach me to ride it. For the rest of that day, I sat by the fireplace feeling sad and rejected. However, as I sat and watched the fire leap around the wood in the fireplace and give its warm, radiant light, I knew deep down in my tender young heart that I too would celebrate a Christmas filled with joy someday.

CHAPTER 18

Kool-Aid Days

Church was the only outlet from the farm for Deborah and me. We considered it our recreation. Bible school was a wonderful time for me. I could make something to take home and give to my Grandma Smith! Usually, the gift was a pot holder, which Grandma Smith could certainly use.. "No money in the budget for such nonsense," Grandpa Smith would say if she tried to buy one. I presented the pot holder to her with a big smile on my face Although it didn't seem to impress her that much, it gave me pleasure to be able to give her a gift.

Each child who attended Bible school was expected to bring something for refreshments. I knew Deborah and I were in trouble. Grandma Smith didn't have much to give. Everyone signed up to bring Cokes, cookies, and other treats. I never remember having cookies as a young child; Grandma Smith just never baked them. When the sheet came around to us, the only thing we could offer was a gallon of kool-aid. My face turned crimson red with embarrassment. But to my relief, Ms. Brown, the Bible school teacher, never made us feel bad because we could only bring kool-aid. She just smiled and said, "That's great." However, we could tell the others kids were not looking forward to kool-aid when they had Cokes all week! Somehow Deborah and I survived the kool-aid days. To this day, I don't like kool-aid! Had enough as a child to last me for a lifetime!

CHAPTER 19

Black Patent Leather Shoes

Once a year, everyone with a loved one buried at the church graveyard gathered for a time of fellowship and dinner on the grounds. Decoration, as the event was called, was a great old time for us girls. Some of Grandpa and Grandma Smith's relatives would travel long distances to arrive at the church by Sunday morning. Each family would bring a picnic lunch and flowers to place on their loved one's grave. The singing, eating, and fellowship would last until late afternoon.

At Decoration, Deborah and I would get to sample foods we didn't have on the farm. There was table after table covered with all kinds of food. It was a dinner-on-the-ground-fest! Somehow, I always seemed to go for Grandma Smith's delicious homemade banana pudding. Everything about it was homemade. She would cook it slowly on the old wood stove. The pudding was smooth and cream-filled, with extra-ripe bananas and vanilla wafers. It made my mouth water just to look at it sitting on the table. The children were always at the back of the line. In those days, children waited for the adults to get their plates of food first, to show respect. After they were finished, we were allowed to line up and dig in. We respected the adults in our household or we would be going to the woodshed for a whipping.

Every year, Deborah and I each received a new dress and pair of shoes in the spring before Decoration. Grandma Smith would somehow manage to buy us one dress a year. For some reason, I can only remember one dress. It was the most beautiful dress I had ever seen, with beautiful blue lace lining the collar. That dress made an impression that is still with me today. My shoes were made of shiny black patent leather. I was so proud of my outfit! I was careful with my dress and shoes, knowing they would be the only ones I would have to wear to church all year.

One Sunday when I took my shiny shoes out from under the bed before church, I saw that they had become dull. It was very upsetting to me, because I had tried so hard to keep them looking new. What would I do, with no polish to bring back the shine? Running to Grandma Smith, I asked if there was anything I could use to shine my shoes with.

"Child, you know we don't have any shoe polish. You will have to wear them to church like they are," Grandma Smith said.

"But Grandma Smith, my shoes are all scuffed up, and I want them to be shiny again," I said. She took me by the hand and led me to the back porch, with one shoe in one hand and one of her homemade biscuits in the other. To my amazement, she split the biscuit in half and started shining the top of my shoe with it. The shoe looked brand new again!

"Now," she said, "Shine the rest of your shoe and the other one, and they will look like new again." She was so right! The homemade lard in my Grandma Smith's biscuit made my shoes look like new. I walked proudly into church wearing my shiny black shoes and my lace-collared blue dress.

Grandma Smith made flowers for the graves of those who had passed on. She would spend weeknights cutting out red, yellow, white, and blue rose petals from crepe paper. The stems were made of wire wrapped with green crepe paper. Her finished project would be a beautiful rose. Most people by then were buying flowers for their loved ones' graves, but not Grandma Smith. She faithfully started making flowers months before the Decoration so she would have enough to place on all of her family's graves.

One year, I asked if I could help her with the flowers. She answered, "Child, you can't do this. You'll just make a mess. Go outside and play." I remember leaving feeling rejected because she thought I couldn't make flowers. Grandma Smith never had much confidence in my ability to do anything but work in the corn field—and even then Deborah and I would receive some criticism. Nevertheless, there did come a day when Grandma Smith would let me help with the flowers, and I was so proud of myself. My first one wasn't the prettiest flower I had ever seen, but I tried hard to please Grandma Smith. She suggested that I roll the green crepe paper on the wire for the stem while she would do the flower. I was happy to be helping. When I finished rolling paper onto the wire, Grandma Smith showed me how to wet the end of the paper with spit so it wouldn't come off. That was cool! I could spit and not get into trouble.

After a short time, Grandma Smith would get tired of trying to help me and tell me to go on outside. On many occasions I would plead with her, only to find a switch around my legs. "Get on out of here now. You have delayed me enough," she would say. You had better believe I was up and out of there in a flash.

I would go outside whispering under my breath, "I hate you." Thank God she never heard me, or she would have switched my legs until I had blood running down to my ankles. Grandma Smith had a lot on her plate and little tolerance for a curious blond-headed girl. I often wondered how I would ever learn how to make the flowers if she didn't let me observe her making them.

Upon our arrival at church, Grandma Smith would take big buckets of her homemade flowers out of the trunk of Uncle Sam's car and place some on each grave. Sometimes if one of the graves didn't have flowers on it, Grandma Smith would take some of her homemade flowers and place them there. "No grave should be without flowers on Decoration," she would say. The graveyard always looked beautiful on that day of the year. When you stood on the hill opposite the graveyard, it beamed with all the colored flowers. It was a sight to behold. Nonetheless, the day always ended much too fast for me. Sadly I knew the next day would be spent working in the hot sun, and I didn't look forward to that.

CHAPTER 20

Don't Go Near the Water

We had little fun on the farm. I can remember on some of those hot Saturday afternoons sneaking to the old swimming hole. It was a cool, refreshing place where the church baptized new converts. Actually, that is where Deborah and I were baptized. She and I had "gone forward" at Bible school when the fire and brimstone preacher finished his message to a young crowd of children about going to hell. I really didn't understand everything he was talking about, but what he said scared me so bad I went forward almost running. All I knew was that I didn't want to go to the place he was talking about. I'd had enough hell in my life being rejected by those in my family. Pastors then didn't sugarcoat anything. They preached hard and plain until you got the message: "turn or burn!"

The swimming hole had a little sandy beach that overlooked a calm bend in the river. All the children from the holler would meet there. Deborah and I had to pretend we were going to our Cousin Martha's house. Grandma Smith didn't like us being at the river. She said, "Don't go near the water until you learn how to swim!" Thinking back, how in the world were we going to learn how to swim if we were never allowed in the water? I guess she was worried we might drown, though I don't know why, given that we always seemed to be an inconvenience to Grandpa Smith and her. If only girls showed up at the swimming hole, we went skinny dipping. When the boys were there, we tied our dresses in knots between our legs before going into the river. We had no bathing suits, so it was in the skin or in the dresses. Grandma Smith didn't allow us to wear pants or shorts. Pants were for boys and shorts were only worn by loose women, according to her.

We had fun in the cool, refreshing water on sunny days. Sometimes we would spend most of the afternoon there. Nevertheless, we always had to leave enough time to lie out in the sun so our clothes and hair would dry. Going home with wet clothes and hair would mean a whipping for sure!

In the old swimming hole, I learned how to dog paddle. I was afraid, but I figured that if a dog could swim, then so could I. In the back of my mind I could hear Grandma Smith's voice saying "Don't go near the water until you can swim." However, desire overruled fear in this case, so out in the water I would run to play. We got lazy days off from the farm work when Grandpa Smith had to go to town. It stayed fresh in our minds that if our cousin Martha were to tell Grandma Smith what we were up to, we would be in a heap of trouble.

One day we were playing away in the water, when we suddenly heard a voice coming from the sandy bank of the river. "Girls, what you doing in that water?", said the voice.

There on the river bank stood Grandma Smith with a big tree branch in her hand. Fear filled our eyes as Deborah and I looked at each other. "Get out of there and take your medicine," she said. Her "medicine" was a tree limb to our legs. We slowly walked to the bank of the river, trying to delay the whipping.

"Didn't I tell you not to go near the water until you could swim?" she said.

"Yes, Grandma," we replied, "But …" That was all we got out of our mouths before the whipping began! Deborah broke loose, but Grandma Smith still had me by the arm. I was running around in circles trying to get ahead of the switch.

"You'd better stand still," she said. *Stand still?* I thought to myself. *The woman's about to kill me!* It seemed I was the one who received the worst whipping. Deborah always managed to break loose, leaving me to take the brunt of Grandma Smith's anger. She finally let go of me. Deborah and I started running up the road to our house. My legs were bleeding, and I had big welts that rose on the skin of my legs. I carried the scars of that day for a while. We didn't go back to the river for a long time. But like most children, we eventually forgot the pain of that day. We began to sneak back to the old swimming hole again for a day of refreshing swimming. At the time, it seemed worth the risk. After getting caught, we were more careful. We always kept a watchful eye on the road that led to the old swimming hole. To my knowledge, Grandma Smith never found out we were brave enough to go back without her permission. I thank God today she never found out, because the price we would have paid would have been much too high.

CHAPTER 21

Feeling like an Ugly Duckling

Deborah was a lovely teenage girl. I always said she looked like Elizabeth Taylor. Her skin was smooth and radiant. She had long, dark, silky hair and a nice figure. I always told her she could only marry Elvis Presley. She seemed to be put together just right, with looks, brains, and personality. I, on the other hand, had dirty blond hair, pale skin, and skinny legs. I always felt like I had big teeth and a forehead only a mother could love—except I never felt I was truly loved by my mother. Maybe it was just me, but I always had the feeling I was the ugly duckling in the family. I heard little remarks on a daily basis about how I looked. No one would give me the time of day. I really felt like I was just an ugly kid no one wanted around. It seemed to me that Deborah could have worn a sack over her head and still looked better than me. It appeared in a little rejected girl's eyes that she was Aunt Neil and Uncle Ned's favorite niece.

As a young child I continued being a thorn in Deborah's side. She didn't like me much because Grandma Smith always made her take me wherever she went. I began to realize Deborah's rejection was attributed to her dislike of me being Grandma Smith's little spy. I can remember following her when she visited our cousin Betty. She would turn and call me mean names. However, that didn't faze me. I would keep on following her. Deborah would become even angrier, and if I happened to be walking too close behind her, she would pick up stones and begin throwing them at me and telling me to go home. On several occasions she hit me with the stones, but I was good at dodging them, so most of the time I would laugh and keep on following her.

It wasn't a laughing matter to Deborah. She would do everything possible to get me to go home. She knew if I followed her that I would tell Grandma Smith everything she had done. I was Grandma Smith's little tattle-tale, and I was very good at it. Each day, I lived to tell Grandma Smith about everything Deborah did, because she was so mean and ugly to me. "Someday I will be taller than you, and I am going to beat you up," I told her. I did grow taller, but I never beat her up.

As the years passed, she liked me less and less. She would get all my cousins to make fun of me and call me names so I wouldn't follow them. My cousins would invite my sister to their house, but tell me I couldn't come. I never really understood the reason behind it all. Maybe it was because they were teenagers, and I was a skinny little ugly duckling they didn't want around. We didn't have a TV, but Aunt Bell and Aunt Lucy eventually purchased one. Cousins in both families would invite Deborah to come and watch it with them, but only if she left me at home. I would cry until Grandma Smith told Deborah she couldn't go unless she took me also. She would turn and look at me with those mean eyes and say, "I hate you!"

It seemed through a little sister's eyes that Deborah took pleasure in making my life miserable. It was hard for a little rejected girl to understand the reason behind why my cousins didn't want me to come. I wanted to watch TV too, and I didn't care if they didn't like me! Finally Deborah would give in and let me go, but she wasn't happy about it. Down the road we would go. Deborah always walked an extreme distance in front of me, daring me to get close enough so she could hit me with a stone. It was a love-hate relationship. I loved Deborah and looked up to her for guidance, and she hated me!

Aunt Lucy would buy Deborah gifts of clothes, jewelry, and other items when she became a young teen. She never purchased me anything that I can remember. My clothing would be mostly dresses that Grandma Smith made out of flour sacks with printed flowers. Time after time, I would see Deborah bring home new gifts and wonder why I was left out. Sometimes Grandma Smith would make Deborah share with me. That made her hate me even more, and she made my life a living hell when Grandma Smith wasn't in sight!

Through all of that, I still looked up to Deborah as the most beautiful sister anyone could ever have. I dreamed of someday being as pretty as she was. I was tired of being seen as the ugly duckling. Why did I have to be the one who would struggle, because those in my family made me feel as if I was ugly?

It seemed Deborah was everyone's favorite when she became older. Uncle David, who lived in Atlanta, decided him and his wife Helen would take Deborah in and give her a better life. I could hardly believe my ears when I heard Uncle David tell Grandma Smith he would take Deborah and raise her as his daughter. Even though she treated me badly, I was sad that Deborah might leave me behind. Having her around was better than being alone. I listened intently as Uncle David and Grandpa and Grandma Smith continued their conversation. Finally, I heard Grandpa Smith say Deborah could go! I was devastated.

"No, Deborah, you can't go and leave me behind," I begged.

She just smiled real big and said, "I will be glad to leave you behind, you little tattle-tale." I followed her around all day watching anxiously as she packed her clothes, hoping at any moment she might decide not to leave.

Uncle David came in and told Deborah it was time to go. Tears filled my eyes as she turned and walked out the door, never looking back at me. Deborah was really leaving me behind! I stood on the big farmhouse porch and watched as Uncle David backed out of the driveway. I could see Deborah through the back window. When she turned and smiled, I waved goodbye with tears streaming down my face. She just kept on smiling, with a gesture that said, "See you later! I'm going to go to the big city and have a great life, you little tattle-tale." My heart was broken because I had been left behind, yet again, by someone I loved. She was happy to leave the farm and its hard work for the big life in Atlanta, it seemed.

Life would continue for me on the farm, and so would the long days of hard work! What was an ugly duckling to do? I felt trapped in a life of hard work and negative words, with no place to go. Summer vacation was even harder for me. Deborah was gone! She seemed to have the good life, and there I was, once again left behind. No one wanted to take the ugly duckling as their daughter. No one had time to feel the pain of a little farm girl who felt rejected and alone. Uncle David and Aunt Helen would bring Deborah to the farm occasionally. She seemed very happy and would show off all the new clothes they had purchased for her. Even if she was a show-off, I still wished she would come back home.

Someday I too will be beautiful, and someone will want me, I told myself.

I kept those words in the front of my mind day after day. I knew I had a dream and someday that dream would come true, if I would just hold on for a better tomorrow. Deborah did come back home after a few years, but not how she thought. The story Uncle David told the family, is his daughter was jealous of Deborah and to keep peace in the family he had to bring her back. However, the way he did it was very painful for Deborah! One day after school he picked her up, with all of her clothes in the car. Uncle David drove Deborah to the steps of the Child Protection Services in our small town and dropped her off. Confused and crying Deborah was placed in a foster home. However, when Grandpa Smith found out he went to the courthouse and asked for Deborah to be returned to his home. Thank God they granted Grandpa Smith's request. We never really understood why Uncle David returned her in that manner. Nevertheless, the important thing was Deborah was back with those she knew. Today, Deborah and I are very close and we support each other as if nothing happened between us many years ago. She is my best friend.

CHAPTER 22

Smooth Talking Ted

Like most children I wanted the all-American family with a mother and a father. Or at least, I thought that was what I wanted. My dream was to have what most of my classmates had: a real family lifestyle. I dreamed about my mother coming and getting me so I wouldn't have to work so hard on the farm. If only I had known then what I know now, I would have stayed on the farm—hard work and all.

One Saturday afternoon, Mother and Junior showed up again! She had married, and her new husband Ted was with her. We were all surprised and a little curious, to say the least. Grandpa Smith was a little reluctant at first when Ted reached out to shake Grandpa Smith's hand.

"Where's your marriage license?" said Grandpa Smith.

"Right here," said Mother, handing it to Grandpa Smith. Grandpa Smith looked it over carefully. He raised his eyebrows as only Grandpa Smith could and then he reached his hand out to shake Ted's. Grandpa Smith invited Ted to sit on the porch and talk. Eventually, Grandpa Smith seemed to warm up to the idea that Ted and mother were married. He talked with Ted for hours. He was trying to get as much information as possible while Ted's guard was down. Ted seemed to be sweating a few times as Grandpa Smith pressed him for answers.

Mother, Junior, and Ted continued to visit each week. The relationship grew between Ted and Grandpa and Grandma Smith. I watched Ted carefully. He was a smooth operator when it came to talking with Grandpa and Grandma Smith. He knew just what to say to win them over. Grandpa and Grandma Smith began relying on Mother and Ted to transport them to town and to the doctor. Grandpa and Grandma Smith became more and more dependent on Ted as the days went by. When Ted talked to them, he was as smooth as creamy peanut butter.

Mother and Ted were going to church regularly, and he was actually a deacon in the little country church close to their home. Mother seemed happy for the first time since I had known her. She seemed to have found the soul mate she had been looking for.

One bright, sunny Saturday, Mother, Junior, and Ted came to take Grandpa and Grandma Smith to the grocery store. A car trip to town would be a special treat for me, because Grandpa Smith didn't have a car. Grandpa and Grandma Smith, Mother, Junior, Ted, and I loaded into Ted's car. We were packed in there like a can of sardines, but I didn't care! It was a day away from the hard farm work, and that made me very happy! On our arrival to town we pulled into the busy parking lot of Hampton's grocery store. Everyone piled out of the car like a bunch of honey bees looking for clover. On entering the store, we could see it was packed with shoppers. Grandma Smith and Mother snatched up the last two carts right before someone else came through the door. The store owners were hustling around trying to get customers checked out so they could free up carts.

Grandma Smith gazed down each aisle to see if she could find one that wasn't too crowded. However, it seemed they all were, so Grandma Smith just went headlong down the first aisle she came to. She pushed carts aside to make her way through the crowded store. Some of the ladies didn't like the fact that she had moved their carts, but Grandma Smith just ignored their attitudes and moved on. I stood close to Grandma Smith's side. She looked down at me and said, "Stay close, child, because I don't have time to look for you if you get lost!" I wasn't used to being in a big store (actually it wasn't that big, but to my little eyes, it seemed huge), so she didn't have to tell me twice. The whole ordeal was a little frightening to me!

We finally made it to the checkout counter! While Grandma Smith was checking out, I walked outside to stand by Ted's car until she finished. Ted approached me as I stood in the warm sunshine and watched people go in and out of the store.

"What are you doing, Joyce?" Ted asked.

"I am waiting on Grandma Smith to finish checking her groceries out," I replied.

"Well, while you're waiting, would you like a Coke?" Ted said. What

kind of question was that? I only had milk with meals and kool-aid on occasion! Coke in Grandma Smith's house wasn't a choice.

"That would be nice, but I don't have any money to buy a Coke," I said. Ted reached into his pocket, pulled out some coins, and dropped them into the palm of my hand.

"Run on over to the old Coke machine and buy you a cold Coke," said Ted.

"No; I can't accept the money without asking Grandma Smith," I said.

"Oh, it's okay. I will tell your grandma I gave you the money," he replied. My eyes lit up like a light bulb in a dark room. Smiling from ear to ear, I approached the old drink machine. I placed my money in the slot and pulled out a Coke. Placing the Coke in the bottle opener, I pulled down on the bottle cap. Pop went the Coke when the cap fell off. Wow, that was neat! I excitedly lifted the bottle to my lips and took a great big sip. It was cool, refreshing, and sweet—lip-smacking good! The bubbles popped in my mouth with a refreshing tingle. Man, it was good! (To this day, Coke is my favorite soft drink.) I walked back to the car, where Ted was laughing at my excitement.

"You like it," he said.

"Yes, thank you so much. It is real good," I replied.

"You are welcome. I'm glad you are enjoying it," Ted said.

Grandma walked out of the grocery store door with the bag boy close behind. Ted lifted the trunk lid, and the bag boy placed the groceries inside. Grandma Smith saw me with the Coke and said, "You didn't beg Ted for money to buy that Coke, did you?"

"No, I didn't ask him for the money, Grandma Smith," I replied.

"No, I gave her the money, Ms. Smith," Ted said.

"Okay. I just did not want her begging you for money," Grandma Smith replied.

Grandpa Smith came walking down the street with a bag under his arm. He had gone to the hardware store to buy a few things he needed for the farm. He liked going to the hardware store, because it was the meeting place for all the farmers in the area. They sat outside on empty old kegs to tell tall tales and spit tobacco while their wives shopped.

"I think all you men do is sit out on the street and watch those loose women in short shorts walk by," Grandma Smith said to Grandpa Smith.

"Now, Elizabeth, you know all we are doing is sitting up there shooting the bull while all you women do your shopping. We can't help it if one of those loose women comes by in her short shorts," Grandpa Smith replied.

We piled back into the car and headed home. I sipped on my Coke all the way home. I wanted to make it last, because it might be a long time before I would get another one. While unloading Grandma Smith's groceries, Ted asked me if I would like to go home with him and Mother and spend the night. I looked at Grandma Smith for an answer. She just shook her head no and said, "She'd better stay with us tonight, because we have church tomorrow."

With a little disappointment, I picked up a bag of Grandma Smith's groceries and carried them into the house. I could hear Mother talking to Grandma Smith. Did Mother really want me to go with her? She had always left me behind before! Grandma Smith was still a little hesitant as Ted tried to convince her that I would be fine.

"We will take Joyce to church on Sunday and return her late Sunday afternoon," he said. Grandma Smith finally said yes! I was one excited little girl. With joy in my heart, I ran to pack clothes for church and jumped into the back seat of Ted's car before Grandma Smith could change her mind! Mother had a new home and a new husband, and I was going for a visit. She finally acted like she wanted me to be a part of her life! In the eyes of this little country girl, life was looking good.

Upon our arrival at Mother's new home, I found it was a little weather-beaten outside, but spotless inside. As we entered the living room, my eyes lit up as I notice a TV in the corner._Following close behind Mother into the kitchen, I could see that one of the cabinet doors was open. Sitting on the shelf was a big bag of sugar wafer cookies. They looked delicious!

When Mother opened the refrigerator door, I could see that it was full of tasty things that I rarely had a chance to eat. My mouth began to water. There was a pack of bologna! Grandma Smith always called bologna "poor man's steak." As I looked more closely, I could see cheese, hot dogs, and all kinds of soft drinks. Coke, Pepsi, and lots of others were just waiting for me to taste them! I decided I'd go for the Coke, because it was my favorite. As I continued to look around, I saw a big bag of candy bulging from one of the cabinets Mother had left open. To this wide-eyed girl, it was a feast! I thought I had died and gone to heaven.

Days at Mother's house were spent sitting on the couch watching TV for hours, eating candy and drinking Coke. Man, this was the real deal! The life I had been waiting for had finally arrived. At least, that is how it seemed. Little did I know what this "real deal" of a life would cost me down the road? Each weekend, Mother would ask Grandma Smith if I could spend Saturday night with her and Ted. This eager little farm girl was ready on Saturday to jump into the car to experience more tasty treats and watch TV for hours. I continued to visit, but during the week I still had to stay with Grandma and Grandpa Smith and work on the farm. The lazy days at Mother's house were a relief from the hard work on the farm.

About three months into the weekend getaways, Mother asked if I would like to come and live with her and Ted

"Wouldn't you rather be here? You wouldn't have to work so hard, and we can give you more of life's pleasures," said Ted.

I was ecstatic! Of course I wanted to move in with them. This wide-eyed country girl was ready to experience the big world she had never seen before and taste life's best. This would prove to be the greatest mistake I would make in my life. But at the time, this sounded like a chance for a real family life to a little girl who had felt nothing but rejection.

CHAPTER 23

Bittersweet

Week after week, Mother and Ted continued to take me home with them on Saturday. But somehow Mother seemed to forget to ask Grandma Smith if I could go and live with them. I was beginning to wonder if she and Ted had changed their minds. Nevertheless, I was having fun, and I didn't want to rock the boat and push my luck. I was around ten and for the first time I felt like someone really cared about me. So I just kept quiet about the whole situation.

Each weekend at Mother's house, the whole family would go fishing at the creek below their house or go for a picnic in the mountains. It was wonderful having a family to do things with. I was one excited young lady. However, late afternoon on Sunday would come around, and it would be time to return to Grandma Smith's house. Mother could tell each time she dropped me off at the farm that sadness filled my face. However, she and Ted never said a word to Grandpa and Grandma Smith about me moving to their house. Feelings of rejection started invading my heart once again. Had they really changed their minds?

Just when I thought they had forgotten about the whole thing, late one Sunday afternoon Mother and Ted sat down on the big farmhouse front porch to talk with Grandma and Grandpa Smith.

"We've been talking to Joyce about coming to live with us," Mother said. Grandma Smith looked up at me. I dropped my eyes to the ground so I would not make eye contact with her. I could tell that Grandma Smith wasn't keen on the idea.

"I need Joyce here to help Henry and me on the farm," Grandma Smith replied. My heart sank when I saw my chance of having what I thought would be a real family lifestyle slipping away.

Ted continued the conversation. "I know Joyce is a lot of help on the farm, but she needs to be with her mother at this age."

Grandpa Smith spoke up. "She's not going, so enough said."

I continued to stay with Grandma and Grandpa Smith. However, Ted continued to talk with them about me coming and living with him and Mother. One Saturday after Ted had taken Grandpa and Grandma Smith to town, he asked them again. This time Grandpa looked at Grandma and said, "It is up to her."

Grandma walked into the house with tears in her eyes. Mother followed after her. Grandma Smith turned to look at Mother and said, "I knew when I raised her to the point that she could help me you would return and take her away."

"I know, but it is time for me to take on the responsibility of supporting her. She can come back anytime she wants to, and if you need her to help in the summer, she can do that also," Mother said. As I best remember Grandma was silent for what seemed to be an eternity. She glanced over at me with tear-filled eyes. I was standing a short distance from her, waiting for her answer. I held my breath, afraid she would say no.

She finally replied, "Well, if she really wants to go, I guess she can go." My heart seemed to be racing ninety miles an hour. Somehow Ted had convinced Grandpa Smith to let me come and live with them! Before Grandma Smith could change her mind, I ran inside and started packing what few things I had into a brown paper grocery bag. Running swiftly to Ted's car in the driveway, I opened the door and jumped inside. Concerned that Grandma Smith might change her mind and I would have to unpack my things and say goodbye to Mother, I decided to lie down in the seat and anxiously wait for Mother, Ted, and Junior to get in the car. I remember saying to myself, *hurry and come on or she will change her mind.*

Finally, they all came and got into the car. I breathed a little easier, but not until the car was started and we were driving down the road did I dare to sit up and look back. I still see a vision of Grandma Smith standing on the big farm porch looking sad. I guess in Grandma Smith's own way she had really loved me, but just didn't know how to show it. As we drove over the little hill and down the dusty road, Grandma Smith faded out of sight.

All I could see was the dust rising from the back of the car. I was a little sad for Grandma Smith, but not sad enough to go back. I had wanted a real family and an easier lifestyle for so long, and they had finally arrived. That outweighed any feelings of sadness at leaving Grandma and Grandpa Smith.

The drive to Mother's house was bittersweet. I was sad for Grandma Smith, but I was excited for myself. When we arrived, I jumped out, ran in, and unpacked my clothes. When I walked back into the living room, Mother had already turned the TV on. Mother turned and said, "Find a seat, and we will watch a little TV before I cook supper."

I sat down on the far end of the big sofa and settled in to watch the *Andy Griffith Show. A family at last,* I thought. I was so happy to have what my other classmates seemed to have. It was an answer to a young girl's prayer—or at least that was what I thought. Mother gave me a Coke to drink with supper, knowing it was my favorite. We had country style steak and gravy. Man, it was good. I had never had country style steak at Grandma Smith's house. (It would be a dish I would come to hate later, because we had it every week. To this day, I hate country style steak.)

I was excited to settle into my new life and was looking forward to going back to school to tell everyone I had a complete family, just like them!

CHAPTER 24

Guest Bedroom

That first summer I did return to work on the farm. I wasn't very happy about it, but I didn't have a lot of say in the matter. I was instructed to go, with no back talk. While I was packing, Ted promised I could come home for the weekends if I would go without complaining. Although coming back sounded good to me, I didn't want to go in the first place. All I saw was hard work in the hot sun. That was the one thing I was trying to escape from.

When I arrived on the farm, Grandma Smith told me to take my clothes to the guest bedroom. Deborah and I had never been allowed to sleep in that room before, so this took me by surprise. Why was she letting me have the room that had been off limits before? Nonetheless, it was a delight to be able to sleep in this room. The room had always been reserved for those most important in Grandma Smith's life. Had I all of a sudden become important? Grandma Smith never told me why she let me sleep in the off-limits room, and I didn't dare ask. I just enjoyed having a room by myself.

Morning would arrive much too early. Grandma Smith called me for breakfast. I rubbed my sleepy eyes and jumped out of bed. I could smell Grandma Smith's fried fatback swirling through the air. She always fried fatback so she could make her country gravy from the drippings. One of her big homemade country biscuits and a couple of spoonfuls of gravy would make your mouth water!

As soon as we had eaten breakfast and washed the dishes, it was time to milk the cows and feed the livestock. I sure didn't miss this when I was at Mother's house. Shortly after that, we headed for the field to cultivate the corn. Some days were so hot and dry I really wanted to walk the ten miles to Mother's house and say, "I'm not going to work on that farm anymore. I hate it!" Nevertheless, something kept me there. Probably fear! I knew if I returned to Mother's, I stood the chance of getting a switch laid to my legs in the worst way. That was enough incentive for me to stay.

One day when Grandma Smith and I were waiting for Grandpa Smith to plow up the ground around the corn, Grandma Smith began to talk to me. "I can't do all this work by myself. I need help. If you will come and help me, I will pay you a small amount," she said. Grandma Smith was drawing social security now, so she had a little money to spare.

Man, I thought to myself. *She is going to pay me for working in the field. Never thought I would see that day!* I had been free labor as far back as I could remember. I really felt sorry for Grandma Smith, but I knew in my heart I was not going to continue to work on the farm. I had worked so hard before that I was just burned out with the whole farming deal, even with money being offered.

That whole summer I worked in the fields while the sun beat down on my head. All of this for a dollar a day from sunup to sundown! However, five dollars a week was better than nothing. It was nice getting a little spending money, but this was neither what I wanted to do nor where I wanted to be. Life was much easier at Mother's house. I didn't want to be in the hot sun cultivating corn. I wanted to go to Mother's house and lie on the sofa watching TV and eating potato chips. I couldn't wait until the weekends rolled around. However, every Sunday night I knew I had to return to hard work and the hot sun. Didn't sound very appealing to me, and I would be glad when it was over. The summer finally ended, and it was time to return to Mother's house before school started.

CHAPTER 25

Forbidden Lie

Summer was at an end, and I wasn't very happy about returning to school, because my whole summer had been no fun, just hard work. Anyway, I knew the teacher would ask everyone where they had gone on vacation. What was I to say? The corn field?

The first day of school went just as I had expected. We filed into the room, and each of us took the seat that had been assigned to us. I always seemed to be placed by a boy who gave me a hard time. While we settled into our desks, the teacher, Ms. Grooms, started asking about vacation sites we had visited. Staring into space with a blank look on my face, I began to roll over in my mind what I would say. I knew for sure I couldn't say, I had spent the whole summer working in the cornfield on Grandpa and Grandma Smith's farm. Everyone would make fun of me! What was I to do?

Listening intently as each classmate described where they had gone on vacation, I was sweating bullets, I hoped that Ms. Grooms would pass me by. The other students had gone to the beach, been camping, and visited other fun places I had never heard of. When my turn came, I froze with fear of being laughed at or ridiculed.

"Joyce, did you go anywhere you would like to share with the class?" asked Ms. Grooms. I choked back the tears. I should have said no. But like most children, I said yes slowly.

"Well, then share with your classmates," Ms. Grooms replied. My mind was racing two hundred miles an hour. I blurted out without thinking, "My new family and I went to the beach!"

I could not believe those words had fallen out of my mouth. Why in the world had I said that? I knew it wasn't true! Sliding down in my desk in fear she would ask me to describe the event, I sat silently. I had never been to the beach and had no idea what it was like. As I think back now, Ms. Grooms must have known I hadn't been, because without asking for details she moved to the next person!

"Thank God," I said under my breath with a sigh of relief. As she continued around the room, I choked back the tears of shame, because I had done the forbidden: lied. As I slumped at my desk, I remembered Pastor Brown's sermon the previous Sunday. "Thou shall not lie, or you will go to Hell for lying" were his words. I was so afraid I would die and go to Hell before the next Sunday morning arrived. At that time it was drilled into your head that you had to be in church to repent and receive forgiveness. You had better believe I was a worried little country girl! Thankfully, I made it until Sunday without dying, and as soon as the altar call was made at the end of the service I was out of my seat. The fact is, I almost ran to repent. I never told anyone that day why I had gone to the altar. I just cried and cried until I felt God had forgiven me.

I was glad to have a new beginning without worrying about the lie I had told. With hope in my heart, I returned to school on Monday praying no one would ask any more details about my so-called vacation. Fortunately for me, neither Ms. Grooms nor my classmates ever asked me about my made-up vacation. I was relieved, and now I could settle into a new year of school with a clean slate.

CHAPTER 26

A Final Goodbye

When I was eleven and a half, Roger, my biological father, appeared out of nowhere, requesting to be a part of my life. I wasn't very happy about the whole situation, but tried to make the best of it. After all these years I finally had a real family, and he showed up yet again acting like he cared.

One Saturday afternoon, Junior and I were playing in the front yard. A car pulled into the driveway and out stepped Grandma Smith with someone we didn't know. As Grandma Smith approached me, she said, "Joyce, this is your daddy and his new family. He would like to see you."

As our eyes met, fear filled my heart. Was he here to mess up my new life, after all these years? Should I run again or stand there and listen to what he had to say? Confused and afraid, I reluctantly walked over to Roger and said, "Hello."

Cautiously, he introduced me to his wife and their children. I guess after the last experience, he wasn't going to make any sudden moves. I gazed at them with my big blue eyes, as surprised as they were.

"Where's your mother?", Grandma Smith said.

"She's in the house," I replied. Roger and Grandma Smith went in to speak with Mother. I ran over and sat down on the porch close to the screen door, trying to hear what they were saying. Roger's wife and children came and sat down in the swing. With fear in my heart, I listened and peeped through the screen door. Mother came out of the door. Roger, Grandma Smith, and Ted were following behind.

"Joyce, your father would like for you to go home with him tonight. Would you like to go?" Mother asked. I was afraid to say no, but also afraid to say yes. What was I to do? I really didn't want to go, yet at this point I really didn't want to hurt his feelings.

After standing frozen in my tracks for what seemed hours, but was only minutes, I answered, "Mother, I really don't want to go." Once again I saw that same hurt and disappointment I had seen many years earlier in Roger's face. I really felt sorry for him, but not enough to go home with him!

Silence was broken by his voice. "Joyce, would you consider going with me to take your Grandma Smith back home? We will stop at the store and get you a treat," he said. With a little hesitation, I agreed to go.

As I slowly entered the backseat, it was evident that the car was small, and we would be jammed in like a can of sardines. I was sitting halfway in the lap of one of Roger's other children. The car was a convertible of some kind. All I remember was that a broom handle went across the top of the car holding the rag top up. We sure were a sight, swaying from side to side jam-packed in an old, run-down car.

Roger took Grandma Smith back to the farm. On our way back, he stopped at Carson's old country store and bought all of us an ice cream treat, as he had promised. We sat on the old porch at the country store and ate our ice cream. The conversation continued about me visiting him and his family. I wasn't the least bit interested in anything he had to say, because in my eyes he had given up his rights the day he left us behind. I don't recall much about the conversation, because frankly at that time he was the one person I didn't want to see. We finished our ice cream and piled back into the old car to head for my house. As we pulled into the driveway of Mother's house, I felt a little relieved. Sitting in the car with what I considered a strange man and his family was making me feel a little uncomfortable.

Roger kept pushing me for answers I wasn't willing to give. After sitting there for a few minutes, I said, "I need to go inside." He turned and handed me a box, saying that if I ever wanted to come to his house, I should let him know. I opened the box a little, revealing a dress. I thanked him and said my goodbyes. He said he would be in touch. As he drove away in that old run-down car, I ran into the house. Mother asked me what was in the box. I opened it and showed her the dress. It was pretty, but when I looked more closely at the size I could hardly believe my eyes. It was a size six child's dress! I was so mad when I saw how small it was. I was eleven and a half years old and wore a size twelve dress. What did he mean by giving me something so small? Did Roger think I was still that little girl he had left behind at four?

Ted started making fun of me and the dress Roger had given me. For some reason he wanted to make Roger look bad in my eyes, and it worked. Weeks later I received a letter from Roger giving me his address. Ted helped me write a letter to Roger and gave me the money to ship the dress back. That would be a day I would regret. I told Roger that I didn't want to ever see him again, and that he should never send me a gift that was too small. I was a young lady now and not a baby. I didn't want him to be a part of my life now or ever! I had a real family and there was no room for him.

Looking back, it seemed a little cruel that I rejected the efforts of a man trying to make up for a mistake he made many years earlier. Nevertheless, at the time it seemed to be the right thing to do. Years later I would come to regret mailing the letter and returning the gift. Roger wrote one final letter. He said, He was sorry that I felt the way I did. He would not try to see me again if that was my wish. It would be his final goodbye!

Well, that's fine with me, I said to myself as I ripped his letter into pieces. Yet in the back of my mind, I wondered if I had made the right decision. Only time would tell, and I had a family now, so why should I need him?

That was the last time I saw Roger. He never made another attempt to see me or contact me as I grew into adulthood. To this day, I have no idea if he is alive or dead. Many times I have wondered where he was and if he ever thought of me. Nonetheless, I never had the courage to contact him in any form. I was afraid the actions of a young child many years earlier had created damage beyond repair. Even as an adult, I would yet again let fear of rejection and pain keep me from trying to salvage a relationship with Roger.

Closure Came

While writing this story, I decided to search for my father. I felt in my heart that he might still be out there. Even if he had died, I wanted to know so I could have closure. I searched for two days with no results. Then I e-mailed an organization with the only information available. They sent me to a website, saying that it might be able to help. I wasn't sure what I would find, if anything. It seemed my father had dropped off the face of the earth without a trace.

Typing in the information I had for him brought me no results. Discouraged, I was about to give up. Then I searched for deaths, and up popped an obituary from a newspaper. A man with my father's name and age had passed away a few months earlier. Could it be him? Had I waited too long?

The search did end that day. I had waited too long. The report I received said, he had been very sick and had Alzheimer's. Even if I had found him months earlier, he probably would not have known me. I guess I was spared the heartbreak of having to see him in that condition, because all memories of me had vanished. I was told by a family member that he had searched repeatedly for me with no results. His desire was to have a relationship with his daughter. Those words gave me peace beyond understanding. Roger really did love me in his own way. Knowing he did search for me and longed to know me was enough. That gave me peace to move forward with closure.

CHAPTER 27

Best Friend

There came a time that I would have a best friend in school. She was a wonderful friend who stuck close to me throughout the year. It was exciting to have that one person who loved me just as I was. Most of my teachers and classmates were never very friendly toward me, but Maggie was different than most. Maggie would make a point to come at play period to talk with me and ask me to play with her. I was surprised because at that time she was considered the upper class. *Why did Maggie want to befriend this little country girl?* I wondered. Nevertheless, I never got up the courage to ask because I was too excited that Maggie called me her best friend! Our friendship grew as the year progressed. I was feeling much better about myself and life in general.

One day, Maggie asked me to spend the night with her. Joy filled my heart! Someone truly wanted me to come home for a visit. I told Maggie I would have to ask my Mother, and I would let her know the next day. As soon as the bus pulled up to my house, I jumped off and ran into the house. Reluctant to ask, because I was afraid Mother would say no, I first took my books to my room. As I approached the kitchen, I could see she was preparing supper. *This would not be a good time to ask. I will wait until she is not so busy,* I told myself.

She turned and asked, "What do you want?"

I felt my blood rush to my head. She didn't like for me to go the houses of families she did not know. Knowing I would have to plead my case, I wasn't ready to confront her with my request. I asked if she needed me to bring in additional wood for the cook stove. She said yes, and I departed to the wood pile, waiting for the right time to ask. After supper, the whole family was sitting on the sofa watching TV. I started to ask, but the words wouldn't come out. Fear was holding me back!

Finally I blurted out, "Can I go home with Maggie, my new best friend?"

Mother didn't even think about my request before she said, "No. I don't know them."

"But Mother, she is my best friend, and she is so kind to me," I said,

"No! You are not going," she replied.

"Please, Mother," I started pleading.

"I don't want to hear any more about going home with this Maggie. I said no, and I mean no," Mother said. However, I wasn't willing to give up, so I continued to plead my case. After a few minutes, Ted asked who she was. When I told him, he said, "I know her dad. He is a good man."

"Well, can I go home with her?" I said.

"We'll see. It's time for bed," said Mother. With fear and tear-filled eyes, I went to bed, hoping and praying she would say yes tomorrow.

First thing next morning, I asked her again. She finally agreed. Joyfully, I got on the bus and left for school. I could hardly contain my excitement until Maggie showed up. Her mother always drove her to school, so I was waiting for her on the sidewalk in front of the schoolhouse. When she pulled up, she saw the smile on my face that told her I could go home with her. Maggie and I laughed together with joy as we entered our classroom. It was Friday, and there would be no school the next day. We were excited to stay up late, watch a movie, and eat snacks.

That afternoon, Maggie's mother picked us up in front of the schoolhouse. I was so excited that I could hardly contain myself. My first sleepover at someone else's house! Maggie's house was beautiful. It had all the conveniences—for one, an inside bathroom! We didn't have an inside bathroom, so it was a treat for me not to go outside in the cold. The bathroom smelled like a flower garden, not like the outdoor plumbing we had. The big tub was a sight to see. For the first time I took a bath in a real tub, not a washing tub. Maggie's bedroom had a beautiful canopy bed. It reminded me of something out of a Cinderella book. Then and there I told myself that someday I, too, would have a beautiful home with an inside bathroom.

The night was exciting. We ate Jell-O, chips, and ice cream. We watched TV until late at night and laughed and giggled the rest of the night without anyone yelling at us! The next morning after breakfast, Maggie's mother said it was time for her to take me home. I wasn't the least bit excited about her taking me home. This was the most fun I had ever had, but I knew all good things must come to an end. I also didn't want them to see where I lived. It was an old shack by the road that had never been painted on the outside. Right below the house was our outside plumbing that I sincerely did not want them to see. How would I ever talk my way out of this one? I could lose Maggie, my best friend, because I was poor, and she was rich in my eyes. My heart ached at the thought of losing her friendship. Why would anyone want to be friends with a poor little country girl who didn't even have a bathroom inside?

The drive to my house seemed long and painful. As we came around the curve, I slowly pointed to the old gray house that was very visible from the road. We pulled into the driveway. Mother came out to greet us. She asked if they would like to come in. *Oh no*, I thought. *Please don't come in.* The house was as bad looking inside as it was outside, in my eyes, because it had been painted with silver paint Ted had found in the dump. What Ted didn't know was the paint would never dry, because it was not made for wood. Each time you brushed against it, you got silver paint on your clothing! What a mess it had become.

Thankfully, Maggie's mother declined. Slowly I got out of the car and told Maggie goodbye. I was so embarrassed and humiliated that I wanted to crawl into a hole and pull dirt over my head. What do they think of me now? Would Maggie's mother still let us be friends?

I braced myself for the worst on Monday morning at school. However, to my surprise Maggie seemed to treat me the same way as before. However, she never asked me to spend the night with her again. I asked her to spend the night with me once, and she said her parents would not let her. I guess she was not comfortable going to an outside bathroom. Besides that, the only heat we had was from a big pot-belly stove in the living room. The rest of the rooms were cold and drafty. She was accustomed to a bathroom inside, an electric stove to cook her meals, oil heat, and a TV in her room. I could not offer any of those conveniences, so she never came to my house to spend the night. It made me sad, but I was glad Maggie was still my best friend.

The school we attended was in town. On occasion she and I would sneak up town at lunchtime to go to the store. However, we knew if we were caught we would be in big trouble. Yet we must have thought it was worth the risk. I will never forget the day we got caught as long as I live. We were almost safe and on school grounds as we rounded the corner. Suddenly, we heard a voice call out to us. We looked at each other with fear. It was the principal, Mr. Rice! He was a mean man who ruled with an iron fist. We knew we were in big trouble. We walked slowly toward him, expecting the worst.

He said, "Girls, where have you been?"

We almost choked on our words as they came out. "We went up town to the store," we answered. "Well, girls, you know you are in trouble for going without permission," Mr. Rice said.

We nodded our heads yes, remaining silent. I was so afraid. If Mother found out, I would have a whipping waiting for me at home. In those days, if you got into trouble at school, you were sure to have another whipping waiting for you when you returned home.

Mr. Rice said, "Go to your classroom. I'll deal with you later." Fear struck my heart like a knife. Would he contact Mother somehow? What was he going to do? Later that afternoon, Mr. Rice appeared at the classroom door. I looked at Maggie, and fear filled our eyes. He called Ms. James, the teacher, outside. They closed the door behind them as we sat silently in our seats. In a few minutes, Ms. James opened the door and motioned for me to come outside. Tears filled my eyes as I slowly pulled myself up and headed for the door. As I entered the hall, Ms. James went back inside and shut the door. There I was, standing by myself with an angry-looking Mr. Rice. He questioned me on why we had disobeyed the rule about going up town without permission. I had nothing to say. He became agitated.

"Answer me," he said.

I raised my head and looked him straight in the eyes. "Sir, I am not the only one who disobeyed this rule. Why are you singling me out with all these questions?" I said.

His face became red as blood, and before I knew what was happening, he slapped me across the face as hard as he could. I fell backward, bumping my head against the wall. At that point he must have realized what he had done.

"Go back into your room. I will deal with you later." he said.

Rejected and feeling abused by yet another male in my life, I walked back into the classroom crying uncontrollably, with a red handprint on my cheek. Ms. James looked up, and her mouth fell open in disbelief. I turned and walked back to my desk. Mr. Rice motioned for her to come outside in the hall. She left the room and stood in the hallway with the door shut, talking with the principal. Maggie was furious.

She said, "I went too, and so did some of our other classmates. Why is he picking on just you?" I could not answer because I was still crying. My face and head hurt, and I didn't understand what had just happened. Deep down in my heart, I felt rejected and abused by another male in my life.

Ms. James entered the room. Her eyes glanced my way, but not a word was said. Mr. Rice left without speaking to Maggie or anyone else involved. He had singled me out as a troublemaker, and I had paid a dear price for everyone. To this day, I get red hot mad when I think about how he treated me. He had gotten away with slapping me across the face without facing any consequences for his actions from the school board. When I told Mother what had happened, she stood up for me for once. My understanding is she told him if he ever laid a hand on me again, she would personally take care of the situation. He never again said anything to me, nor did he confront me about anything else. I guess Mother put the fear of God in him.

Maggie and I would remain friends for the rest of the year. Oh, how I cherished her friendship. The other classmates seemed to accept me as their friend because of Maggie. That made me have a little more confidence. However, that would soon come to an end, because we were never classmates in later years. I don't know if that was initiated by Mr. Rice or her parents. Still, Maggie always spoke to me when she met me in the hall or if we happened to be in the bathroom at the same time. Maggie was truly a good friend, who looked past the poverty of a dirty farm girl and accepted me right where I was. A true friend is hard to find, and I will forever cherish the memories of her.

Maggie Was Gone

A few years later, after I left the small town where I had lived and moved in with Deborah, I picked up a paper, and there on the front page was Maggie's picture. She became pregnant at the young tender age of seventeen. She married the young man, and they were living with her parents. The marriage only lasted for a short period. "Too young," was the verdict I heard.

One dark cold winter night as Maggie returned home, she was gunned down in her parent's driveway by her jealous ex-husband! My heart sank as I continued to read the story. My kind friend Maggie had lost her life at a young tender age. I couldn't keep back the tears of pain as I stood there shaking in disbelief! Not my best friend Maggie, who a few years earlier had shown this little country girl so much kindness. I could not make myself go to the funeral. I wanted to remember Maggie as the girl she was when she and I had laughed together and played together—and the one who was so kind and caring! There is not a doubt in my mind that she received a reward in heaven from God for befriending this little country girl. When I get to heaven it will be my opportunity to sit down with Maggie and tell her how much I appreciated her friendship and love. I know we will have a wonderful time getting reacquainted. My friend Maggie will live forever, in my heart.

CHAPTER 28

The Wrong Move

There came a time when Ted started drinking excessively. First it was binge drinking on the weekends. He would start at noon on Saturday after taking Grandpa and Grandma Smith to town and continue until seven p.m. on Sunday. Ted continued this until one weekend he had a car accident. He was out with his drinking buddies one Friday instead of working, driving from a package store where they sold beer. When they came around one of the steep curves in the road, another car came around the curve on the wrong side of the road and ran them down an embankment. After being hospitalized, Ted turned out to have a broken leg and a broken arm. It was a blessing he was still alive.

Even though God had spared his life, it seemed from his actions that he was not thankful. The weeks that followed would prove to be the worst drinking binge I would ever encounter. Ted seemed to have lost all desire to do anything except drink. At that point, he and Mother were not attending church. Everything went downhill. Shortly after the accident, the insurance company paid Ted a lump sum of money. I think it was around four thousand dollars. That was a lot of money in those days. Nonetheless, it would be the beginning of a drinking binge that lasted three months. Every day when I came home, he was well on his way.

The only time he sobered up was for Saturday morning, so Grandpa and Grandma Smith would not know he was drinking. However, as soon as he returned from the farm he would start drinking again. Ted was the meanest man I knew when he was drinking. He began to call me ugly names and threatened to slap me if I talked back. I really didn't understand what I had done wrong. But, fearful that Ted would follow though with his words, I would go to my room or out on the porch to get away from him. Sometimes silence was the better strategy for me to use. The road that seemed so straight and safe had become a road of horror for a young girl who had placed all her hope for a brighter future in Mother's new husband, Ted.

We continued to do things as a family, but he was always drinking. Not long after the accident, Mother started drinking with him. They left me home to babysit Junior. They were gone for hours at a time, and I never knew when they might return or how to get in touch with them if something happened to Junior or me. When the wind howled around the old gray house, it shook, and the creepy sounds sent chills down my spine. I was so afraid at times I wouldn't move and would turn the TV up as loud as I could to drown out the noise. Sometimes, I would fall asleep, and Mother and Ted would walk in without my noticing. Then I would be fussed at for being up too late and having the TV on too loud. My only escape from the verbal abuse was to go to my bedroom and shut the door. However, Ted would threaten to kick the door in and kick my behind. When Mother heard me crying, she would somehow get Ted under control and in bed. That was a relief for me. I never knew what he was capable of when he was three sheets in the wind.

On Sundays, I walked to church with Junior. It was instilled in me by Grandpa and Grandma Smith at a young age that you must go to church on Sunday. My grandparents' Christian roots would give me strength to go on even in the roughest time of my life. As I recall, going to church was probably the one thing that helped me keep my sanity.

The drinking continued as long as the money lasted, and so did the abusive language. I was told if I said anything to anyone about what was going on in that household, I would pay dearly. So I kept my mouth shut and pretended everything was okay. I played the role well, because no one expected anything. I was not accustomed to anyone drinking in my presence. I never saw Grandpa Smith drink any kind of alcoholic beverage. This was all new to me. Afraid and confused, I kept to myself as much as possible. The house became even more rundown, but Ted didn't seem to care. One night a hard rain came, and we had to place buckets everywhere because the roof was leaking so badly. He did repair the roof after that. However, other repairs were left undone. The house became dilapidated and had the appearance of an old, weather-beaten shack. What had I gotten myself into? I must have been crazy. Going back to Grandpa and Grandma Smith wasn't an option, as Ted constantly informed me whenever I said anything about returning.

"You're here and you will stay here," he said. I found myself in a dangerous situation, with no hope of anyone rescuing me. I had rolled the dice and made the wrong move. After the insurance money ran out, Ted returned to work. His daily drinking would have to end on weekdays, because he would lose his job. Nevertheless, when work ended on Friday he stopped by the package store and bought a six-pack of beer. He didn't drink too much on Friday nights, because he had to take Grandma Smith to the grocery store the next morning, and if she smelled alcohol on his breath she would chew him out. He didn't want Grandpa and Grandma Smith to know he was drinking, so he kept it hidden well. They thought the sun set and rose in Ted. However, if they had known what was going on behind closed doors, they would have disowned him.

After dropping Grandpa and Grandma Smith off from their weekly grocery trip, Ted would drive to another package store to purchase his first six-pack of beer on Saturdays. That was the first of many for the weekend. On some occasions, Ted and Mother would tell Junior and me to come with them, because they planned on going straight to the store and back. Many times Ted would tell mother to stay in the car and he would be right back. However, that right back would turn into hours. Eventually, Mother would go in to get him. But rather than bringing him out, she would sit down and start talking and drinking with him. For hours, Junior and I would sit in front of a bar in the car on cold winter afternoons. It was daylight when we arrived and midnight when we left.

I never dared say anything because I would be slapped across the mouth for back-talking. However, the excessive drinking was producing an unbearable home environment and lifestyle in the eyes of a rejected little country girl. I never knew what was going to happen next. It was like living with a demon with a split personality. Maybe, I would wake up one morning and realize it had only been a bad dream. There was a deep-seated fear always lingering in my mind as to what would happen next in my life. However, Ted had never made any out of the way sexual advances at this point.

Many times Mother insisted that Junior and I go with them for a ride, but it seemed we always ended up in front of a bar sitting in the car.

Because of Ted's excessive drinking, I was forced to drive at a young age. There were many occasions that Ted could barely stand up when he came out of the bar. Ted didn't like me much, but he knew someone had to drive. I had been driving a little in the yard, but not enough to be driving on the road. I was much too young to have my driver's license. Nevertheless, he couldn't drive, so I climbed under the stern wheel of the old car and started driving. I knew I would have to learn how to drive real fast on the open highway. Fear struck my heart that I might be caught driving without a license, but at least I wasn't drunk!

"Oh, God, don't let me get caught driving without a license, and please get us home safely," I remember praying. Somehow, we did arrive home safe. I was so grateful when we turned into the driveway of our house. God was watching over me even when I was breaking the law. Somehow and some way, the Lord protected this little country girl on those dark, lonely back roads. That was the first of many times I had to drive them home after a night of drinking too much. Each time I prayed for protection, and each time we would arrive home safe and sound.

CHAPTER 29

Fairy-Tale Dream Shattered

One Saturday afternoon we all talked about going fishing. Mother didn't really want to go, and Junior was busy playing with the boy who lived up the road from us. We had gone fishing many times before, so this was no different from any other time. At least that was what I thought! Mother suggested that Ted and I go for about thirty minutes while she cooked supper. We didn't have anything to fish with except old cane poles, but they worked well for fishing in the river. I really liked fishing, so I ran excitedly down the path beside our house and dug up some earthworms for bait. These would work just fine for those fish waiting to be caught. After catching them, we would clean them and fry them on the old wood stove in an iron skillet. My mouth could practically taste those fish as I jumped into the car with my cane fishing pole.

It was nice having someone to take me fishing. Even if Ted did cuss and call me names, I did have something of a family. Ted's abuse had never gone beyond words. and I learned how to deal with them somewhat. However, before nightfall that day I would learn what Ted was capable of. Little did I know what lay ahead for this twelve-year-old girl.

We pulled onto a side road that led to the river. Just below the fishing hole was a neighbor who owned the land around the river. He did not mind that we fished on his property. He was a nice neighbor, as I remember. We got out of the car and walked down the embankment where the river flowed in a winding path. It was a cool, relaxing place. There was a deep pool in the bend where we always found fish waiting to bite the worms we placed on our hooks. We had fished there many times before as a family, so I was very familiar with the area.

It was a cool summer day, so the fish would bite well. I sat down on a rock by the river and placed an earthworm on my hook. Ted did the same. Both of us got a bite at the same time. I lost mine off the hook, but he managed to pull his onto the bank. It was a large catfish. Man, he was a big one! Since we didn't eat catfish, he placed the big old catfish back into the water. We were looking for trout to clean and eat. Still, it was exciting to see that big catfish. I couldn't wait to tell Junior what he had missed.

We continued to fish for a while. It was fun, but it came time to go home. I started picking up the can of worms and my cane fishing pole. As I turned to walk up the embankment, Ted approached me. I thought he was trying to help me carry the bait and fishing pole to the car. However, he placed his hands on my shoulders, holding me back. I stood there wondering what he was doing. I said, "You ready to go home?"

"No," Ted said. His grip tightened on one of my shoulders as his other hand slid down my dress, and he started touching me inappropriately. I tried to push his hand away, but he was much too strong. I was frightened beyond my wildest dreams. I remembered what Grandma Smith had told me. If any boy tried to touch me down there, I was to kick him where it would hurt! I raised my leg, just like Grandma Smith had told me, and kicked Ted in the privates. He let go of me and bent over in pain.

I started running like a frantic mad dog up the bank. One more step and I would be out in the open and at the top of the bank. I was crying uncontrollably with fear. Nevertheless, I must not look back but try hard to escape. My plan was to run to the neighbor's house. However, just as I reached the top of the bank, I felt Ted's hand grab my foot. Down I went on my hands and knees as Ted jerked my feet out from under me. I grabbed hold of some small branches that had grown on top of the bank. They came up by the roots, and I felt myself slipping. I grabbed another limb as I continued to hold on with all my power to prevent him from getting his hand on me again. However, Ted was much stronger than me, and I felt myself slipping even farther down the bank. I dug my fingernails into the red clay of the bank, trying to resist his hands. But it was useless to try to hold on. I felt his hand reach higher on my leg. I was still trying to dig my fingers in the red clay bank, thinking that at any moment I might be able to escape his tight grip. Suddenly, he grabbed my other leg and forcefully dragged me the rest of the way down the bank and slung me on the ground. What was he going to do? I remember pleading and begging him to turn me loose. He held my arms even tighter, forcing me against the ground so hard it felt like he was breaking my arms.

I continued to kick with all the power I had left in me, even as he pulled at my panties and ripped them from my body. His breath was hot and smelled like beer. Sweat was dripping from his forehead from his struggle to force me from the bank I had so desperately clung to just seconds before. I continued to struggle to get loose. However, he was so much stronger than me it was of no use. He took both of my arms in one hand and reached for a rock nearby. Would I live to see tomorrow?

He held the rock over my head and said, "I will bash your head in and throw your body in the river if you don't stop kicking." The pain was more than I could bear. I was still sobbing uncontrollably.

"I will tell them you fell into the river and hit your head on a rock," he said. Fearful and trembling, I turned my head to avoid the smell of his breath and the sight of his beady eyes. It was at that point that I cried out as loudly as possible, "God, please help me!"

I started talking as fast as I could about the neighbors hearing me screaming. He must have come to his senses, because he finally stopped.

"I will let you go if you don't run," he said. I would have said anything to get him off me, so I agreed. He loosened his strong grip on my arms. I slowly rolled over to one side, still sobbing with pain. I had red clay all over my face, dress, and body where he had dragged me down the embankment. Still shaking, I slowly regained enough strength to stand up. Ted grabbed my arm again.

"If you tell your mother, I will finish what I started to do. I will kill you, and don't you ever forget that," he scowled.

"Now go wash your face and legs in the river, and get the red clay off. If your mother asks, you tell her you fell in a mud puddle."

Tears were streaming down my face. Ted grabbed my arm again and said, "Shut up that crying and do as I say."

Afraid and not fully understanding what had just taken place, I slowly walked to the river to clean myself up as much as possible. Still afraid that at any time he would follow through with throwing me into the river, I quickly washed my face, legs, and hands. Feeling confusion and pain, I turned to see where he was. Should I run now? Where would I go? Ted motioned for me to come on. He had walked to the car and was waiting.

Slowly, I walked up the embankment, gazing at the deep lines I had dug in the red clay with my fingers.

Ted grabbed my arm again. "You'd better not tell your mother, you hear me?" he said. I shook my head that I would not say anything.

"Get in the car," he said. As I opened the car door, I saw the reflection of my face looking pale, sad, and humiliated in the car window. I sat down in the car with disbelief. How would I ever recover from what had just taken place moments before? I keep my face and body turned away from Ted, looking out the car window. I couldn't stand the thought of being in the same car with this monster.

The drive home took only five minutes, but it felt like an hour. Without showing any emotions, I slowly got out of the car. He gave me a mean look, and I dropped my eyes to the ground. I went straight to my bedroom and changed clothes before Mother could see me. She was still in the kitchen preparing supper and had no idea what had taken place only five minutes from the house. I walked out of the bedroom, went to the front porch, and sat down in the swing. Still shaking from the trauma I had just experienced at the hands of someone I thought cared about me, I sat quietly. I looked down at my hands and saw I still had red clay under my nails. I walked to the back porch, where a bucket of water and a wash pan sat. I took the soap from the dish, scooped up a cup of water, and poured it into the pan. Trying as hard as I could, I begin digging the red clay out from under my nails. Standing there, I had a flashback of what had just taken place and started weeping. I knew somehow I had to tell Mother what happened, but how? Would Ted really kill me if I told her? He said he would. But I couldn't take a chance it might happen again.

Mother called us for supper. I felt sick to my stomach at the thought of sitting at the same table with this evil man! However, I had no other option. I wasn't hungry, so I sat quietly, picking at my food. After supper Mother told me to wash and dry the dishes. I stood at the kitchen sink, looking in the mirror hanging on the wall. My face was still pale, and there seemed to be emptiness in the eyes looking back at me. The whole ordeal had left me shaken, afraid, and in disbelief. *Why me?* Was the question that lingered in my mind? What had I done to deserve this kind of treatment?

Hearing the front door slam, I realized that Ted had walked outside to the outhouse. This would be the chance I needed to tell Mother. Very slowly, I approached her as she stood with her back to me at the stove. "Mother, I need to tell you something before Ted gets back into the house,"

I said quickly. She turned and looked at a fearful child whose voice was shaking.

"What's wrong?" she said.

"Ted is what's wrong," I replied. I began to tell her everything that happened. Mother's face turned red.

"I'll have a talk with him as soon as he gets back into the house," she said. Never once did she take me in her arms for security or comfort. Somehow, I felt only shame and disgrace as I turned to see Ted heading back from the outhouse. *I had better get out of his way*, was my first thought. *Ted will kill me*! As soon as he entered the house, Mother confronted him about the whole issue.

Ted denied everything. "Joyce is trying to cause trouble between you and me. I haven't done anything to her. She is lying through her front teeth." he said. His eyes turned to me, and I slipped behind Mother for protection.

"He did hurt me," I insisted.

She looked at Ted and said, "I don't know who is lying, but you had better never touch her again if this happened." The worst feelings for me were I didn't think Mother really believed me, or else she would have left with me and Junior right away.

Mother told me to drop the whole issue, never tell anyone what happened, and stay away from him when she was not around. This was not what a child who had been rejected all her life wanted to hear. The fairy-tale dream of having an all-American family had just become the worst nightmare of my life.

All fairy tales begin with, "Once upon a time." My fairy tale could have begun with, "Once upon a time, a young blue-eyed girl's life was shattered like a broken mirror by a monster called Ted." Would I ever be able to pick up the pieces and move on? Would Mother really sweep the whole ordeal under the rug as if it never happened? I wanted him to pay for his evil deed! However, in those days, what went on in the home stayed in the home.

How could Mother do this to me? I grew to hate her as much as I hated Ted. I told myself that I would make sure he paid for his evil deeds. I found myself in a dangerous world, desperately in need of someone to rescue me from the hands of a madman! Would anyone step in and help?

CHAPTER 30

Choke Hold of Death

The next few years would be more of the same: abuse, just in a different way. I was so afraid of Ted, and I always made sure I wasn't in the same place with him alone. He hated me as much as I hated him. Mother seemed to wear blinders when it came to him. The old saying "If you pretend it didn't happen, then it will go away" fit her to a T. But in this child's mind, Ted was the devil in skin.

Often, I thought about how I could kill him without getting into trouble. He had turned into a very mean man, and he seemed to get meaner every day. On one occasion, I was sitting in the corner behind the big potbelly stove used to heat the house. Ted looked at me and shook his finger, saying. "You got me in trouble with your mom, and I will pay you back."

"What trouble? She didn't do anything about what you did," I said. Mother was in the kitchen cooking, but I was sitting where she could keep an eye on me at all times. Mother heard Ted talking to me. However, she couldn't hear clearly what he was saying. She came into the room.

"Ted, leave Joyce alone," Mother said.

Ted stood up and shook his finger in mother's facet and said, "Keep your damn mouth shut, woman. I am not doing anything."

I was afraid he was going to hit Mother. I screamed as loud I could, "leave her alone you asshole." He turned and looked at me. His face was blood red. That was the wrong thing for me to say. He ran over to where I was sitting behind the stove, grabbed me around the throat, and pulled me forcefully up out of the chair. I don't know if it was because he had frightened me so badly or because he had pulled me up so fast, but either way, I lost consciousness. When I came to, I was on the floor, and Ted was over me on his knees with a choke hold around my throat. I don't know what happened while I was out, but when I became fully aware of my surroundings, Mother was standing over him with a small piece of wood she used for the cook stove.

Mother yelled loudly, "Turn her loose and leave her alone."

He continued to choke me as if he didn't hear her. It was at that point that she drew back the piece of wood and hit him as hard as she could on top of his head. Ted collapsed and fell on the floor like a dead man. Still gasping for breath, I scrambled to my feet as fast as I could. I was still trembling from the experience, but managed to slip behind Mother for protection. I wasn't sure what was going to happen next. One thing I did know was that I had better seek safety.

Mother told him he had better not touch me again as he laid on the floor rubbing the big knot that had already appeared on his bald head. "Get up and go sit on the couch and leave Joyce alone," she said.

For some reason, Ted didn't talk back that time. He was rubbing his head as blood streamed down his face. He sat up and crawled on his hands and knees to the couch. Mother helped him sit down. Ted's head was swelling more every second, it seemed, and the blood was still streaming down his face. He seemed to be in extreme pain as he rubbed his head again. I was glad because I was afraid he would be coming after me again.

Mother returned to the kitchen to get a bag of ice for his head. He had a headache for days. However, not once did he say anything to me about the whole ordeal. I can say for sure that Mother saved my life that day. Ted had the choke hold of death around my neck, and he did not release me until she popped him upside the head with that stick of wood.

For weeks I walked around on pins and needles. When Mother got up to go to another room, I got up and followed her. If she went outside to use the outhouse, I would go sit on an old stump beside it. I spent as much time as possible sitting in the swing on the front porch. I would wait until it was dark, then slip into the kitchen, wash up, and go to bed. Ted would be gone for work by the time Mother called me to get ready for school. Thank God I didn't have to face him first thing in the mornings. I mostly received the silent treatment from him. That was fine with me, because I didn't have anything to say to him either. He always gave me a look that said "go to hell." My hope was that somehow I would find a way to escape this man I had grown to hate. I was in a fearful place and seemingly on my own. I would have to find my own way out of a dangerous situation.

Ted never had a kind word for me anymore, and when he was drinking he let me have it verbally. I was never allowed to visit my friends during this time. The only place I could go to escape his abuse was the little Baptist church down the road. I would get up early on Sunday morning and walk there alone to seek some peace. I hated it when the pastor said the service was over, because I knew what was waiting for me at home: more abuse. Would this ever end? I continually asked myself what had I done to deserve what was happening to me?_But as time went by, my life would become even more unbearable.

CHAPTER 31

Horror behind the Closed Door

Night after night, I would go to bed wondering if I would be alive the next morning Ted's threats of killing me lingered in my mind each time I drifted off to sleep. The tears I shed in the moments before I fell asleep each night were sad and painful. I would pray each night for God to protect me from the mean, evil man who fooled and deceived everyone else in the family.

Then it happened. I was awakened by the squeaking of my bedroom door. I lay still, afraid to move. Nevertheless, I peeked through my sleepy eyes to see who was coming in. Oh no! Ted was peering through the small crack in the door. Many things ran through my mind as he started into the room. What was he up to? Would this be the day he would end my life, or was more abuse in store for me? I pretended to be sound asleep as he opened the door farther, hoping with all my heart he would turn and leave. However, that would not happen. He slowly walked to the side of the bed and bent down, slipping his hands under the covers. He began by placing his hands on my breasts and then reached down to my panties. I froze and began to shake, not knowing what he would do next. I rolled over, still pretending to be asleep, trying to escape his hands. My mind was going ninety miles an hour trying to decide how to get away from him. Should I scream or make some kind of noise to get my mother's attention? I lay helpless in bed, trapped with an abusive man who would kill me if I made the wrong move.

Mother was in the kitchen preparing breakfast and had no idea what was taking place. Oh, how I prayed she would come through the door and rescue me from the hands of this beast. My prayers were answered when in came Mother.

"What are you doing in Joyce's bedroom, Ted?" Mother asked.

He jumped back, startled by her entering the room, and said, "I came in to wake her up for breakfast."

I looked at mother with fear in my eyes. She looked at Ted and said, "Whatever you were doing, get out of this room and get ready for breakfast now!"

I was relieved that she had come in at the right moment. Unfortunately, it was the first of many mornings that Ted would be brave enough to sneak into my room and fondle me.

I deliberately lingered in my room so I would not have to face him at the breakfast table. However, he seemed to be taking longer than usual to leave for work. Mother called once again for me to come and eat breakfast. Slowly, I walked through the living room and entered the kitchen. Afraid, shaking, and pale as a ghost, I slipped into the chair at the far side of the table. I was so sick to my stomach that I couldn't eat. I sat at the table, once again picking at my food with my head down. No way would I make eye contact with this evil man! I eventually raised my head and glanced over to where Ted was sitting. He glared at me with piercing eyes. I quickly bowed my head and continued to pick at my food.

When Ted finally got up from the table to leave for work, relief filled my heart. I waited anxiously for the car to go out of sight. Now I could talk to Mother and tell her what really happened. However, Ted was a good liar, and she seemed to believe everything he said. More than likely he would convince her I was lying about everything once he found out I had told her why he was in my room.

Approaching Mother, I confronted her with the facts of what Ted was doing in my bedroom. She didn't seem to be surprised, and only said,

"Place something in front of your door to keep him out." That wasn't much comfort for a child who was being abused and threatened!

All day at school, I dreaded going home. What would I face when I got there? Would he threaten me once again? When the school bus pulled up in front of the house, I saw to my surprise that his car was already in the driveway. I had assumed I would have additional time to talk with Mother before he got home, but it seemed he had come back early.

The steps from the bus to the front door felt a mile long. There sat Ted on the sofa, drinking beer. His eyes were already red, and he was well on his way to being drunk. When I opened the front door and walked through, Ted gave me a nasty look. Mother was in the kitchen, so I walked swiftly passed Ted as she turned to greet me.

"Get you something to snack on, because supper is not ready yet," she said. I sat down at the table to eat my snack and do my homework. Anything to stay out of Ted's reach! Mother retuned to the living room and sat down with Ted. After I had lingered around in the kitchen much too long for Ted's liking, he yelled from the living room, "Joyce, get out of that kitchen and cut the lights off. I'm not paying for every light to be on in the house."

I knew if I didn't do as he said, he would cuss me out. So, I slowly got up from the table and turned off the lights. I entered the living room and slipped behind the hot potbelly stove, sitting down in a chair where he could not see my face. Afraid, trembling, and pale, I kept my head down while trying to do my homework by the dim light overhead.

I dared not make eye contact with him, because he was drunk and I knew he could get real mean. Ted seemed agitated to the max! I knew something must have happened while I was at school, but what? Had Mother confronted him about being in my bedroom this morning? All I knew was that Ted seemed mad as a hornet whose hive had been disturbed.

Mother got up and went into the kitchen to start supper. Fear struck my heart. What would he say or do now that she was in the kitchen? I looked up quickly and peered around the big potbelly stove. Ted shook his big finger at me with a gesture that said, "I'll get you later." I quickly lowered my head and pretended to do my homework while he continued to drink his beer. However, I was so afraid I could hardly concentrate. After supper, I washed the dishes and went straight to bed. I couldn't stand to be around him! He made my skin crawl. My dream was that somehow he might be killed in an automobile accident going to work or coming home.

That night, as I was preparing for bed, I looked around for something to put in front of the door to keep Ted out of my room. A table with a small record player was the only thing I could find. I shut the door and placed the table in front of it for added protection. I never knew what Ted would do because he was so unpredictable. I knew one thing: at all costs I must protect myself from this evil beast.

The very next morning, I was awakened by the sound of the table sliding across the floor. I opened my eyes, fearful of what or who I would see. It was Ted! He kept pushing the table a little bit at a time, so Mother would not hear him from the kitchen. What would he do next? Nothing seemed to stop him. This time when I rose up in the bed, there he stood in the doorway with his privates exposed. I panicked and screamed Mother came running through the house. He quickly left the doorway and jumped back into his bed. Their bedroom was adjacent to mine, which made it convenient for him to quickly get back into bed before Mother could catch him standing in the doorway with his privates exposed. I was like a trapped, scared rabbit being chased and cornered by a hound dog! I had nowhere to go if he decided to hurt me, and no one to turn to for help.

Mother asked what was wrong. Ted spoke up and said, "I think Joyce is having a bad dream."

Bad dream?, I thought to myself. *Mother can't you see what is going on here? Or do you really even care?* Somehow, I knew by looking at Mother's face that she wasn't buying his story this time. However, would she do anything to protect her young daughter from the beast she had married? Somehow, I needed to find someone to tell about the daily terrors I was being subjected to. Nonetheless, I felt alone, terrified, and brokenhearted. Leaving for school that morning, I contemplated running away, never to be seen again. But how would I care for myself alone at such a young age? Besides, if Ted found me, the abuse would escalate. As far back as I could remember, I had always been struggling against overwhelming odds.

Every day after school, I would have to return to a house of hell and face what might happen next behind the closed door of my bedroom. When I returned from school one afternoon, Mother was waiting at the door. She took me to my bedroom to show me the lock she had nailed to my bedroom door. I shut the door and locked it, to see how it worked. The only way he could get into my bedroom now was to bust down the door. Relieved that I would have a little more protection, I thanked Mother. She had believed me and was trying to do something to protect me from his abusive hands. Confused and hurt, I still wondered why she stayed with him after being aware of all he was capable of doing at any time.

We always went to bed early. I felt a little more comfortable now that I had a lock on my door, but not completely. I would find out soon that even a lock wouldn't protect me from this sex-crazy man! The next morning, I was awakened by someone pushing as hard as they could against the door. It sounded like Ted trying to enter my bedroom. However, the lock prevented him from coming in without making any noise. Evidently that must have infuriated him, because suddenly he kicked in the door and said, "It's time to get up, you lazy bitch."

I jumped up in bed and started screaming. Mother came running through the house again, screaming at the top of her lungs, "What are you doing? Get out of Joyce's room and leave her alone."

He turned and with wrath in his voice yelled, "She better never put a lock on the doors in my house again."

"Joyce didn't put the lock on her door. I did." Mother replied.

Ted turned and pointed his finger at me, saying, "Get your lazy ass out of bed and get ready for school."

I looked at Mother for help. Mother stepped in and said, "Ted, you go into the kitchen and eat your breakfast. I will take care of Joyce".

Ted was trying very hard to cover up what he was really up to. I could tell Mother saw right through his cover-up attempt. She turned to me and said, "Get ready for breakfast. We will talk later."

Nevertheless, she probably would not do anything other than what she had already done. In my opinion, that was not enough. Many times after that day, he entered my room trying to fondle me. However, Mother kept a close eye on him after he broke down my door. He never got past touching me on my breasts and private area. Nevertheless, I was still afraid of what he might do next. He was a creep in my eyes and I didn't want him near me.

One hot summer night, Ted told Mother he was going to the outhouse. I was already in bed. She was in the living room with the TV on so she couldn't hear clearly. I was startled to see someone standing at my window. They began to rip away at the screen! Afraid to look but more afraid not to, I sat up in bed to get a closer look. It was Ted! Without thinking, I screamed as loudly as I could. He stepped back from the window and started running around the house.

Mother came running into my room. "What in the world is wrong with you?" she said.

"Someone was at my window trying to break in," I replied.

Ted ran into the house, inquiring as to what was wrong. *What was wrong?* I said to myself. *You snake in the grass—it was you who was at my window!*

Ted walked outside, supposedly looking for whoever it was. Ted was a real piece of work when he was trying to cover up his wicked acts! Mother came over and looked out my window. She could tell someone had tried to rip the screen off. She reached over, shut the window, and locked it.

"You will be fine now. No one can get in without breaking the window, and I would hear that," she said. Ted came back in, acting as though he had looked for whoever had tried to break into my room.

"Didn't see anyone; they must have ran when Joyce screamed," he said. How could he be so cool about the whole thing, knowing all the time it was him? Why couldn't Mother see through his lying eyes? I wanted to tell Mother with him standing right in front of us, but I knew Ted would lie yet again, and Mother wouldn't do anything except lay a tongue lashing on him.

Regardless of whether she did anything or not, I felt I should tell her the next morning. I waited until Ted left for work. Entering the kitchen and sitting down at the table, I looked up at Mother and said, "Mother, you do know that Ted was the one trying to get in my room last night?"

She just sighed and said, "I thought it might have been him."

I knew at that moment I was on my own, and somehow I must get out of that house as soon as possible. That was the day I started making plans to escape the abuse I was receiving from the hands of a crazy man.

CHAPTER 32

Living in Fear while Making Plans

I began preparing to find a way to get out of the abusive situation that continued day after day. I was living a fearful life of sleepless nights and days spent walking around the house like a scared rabbit to avoid Ted. I never knew when he would explode like a pack of wild wolves and lash out in an abusive way. Ted was like a walking time bomb waiting to explode at any second. He was hot-tempered and always crossed all boundaries, regardless of who set them. He was an out-of-control madman, in my opinion.

Most days, if Mother happened to be outside, I faced him touching me on my bottom or breast as I walked by. On many occasions he would grab me by my arm and pull me close to him, saying, "I'll get you sometime. Your mother won't always be around."

As I pulled away, the pain of his grip would bring tears to my eyes. On one occasion, Mother was outside. As I entered the living room, I realized she had walked outside to the outhouse. I never slowed down, but continued to walk through the living room to go to the porch until Mother came back. As I walked by, Ted grabbed my dress tail. Rip went the dress as I opened the screen door. "You bitch, come back here," he said.

I never looked back but continued to move out the door, so I would be visible to my mother. Slowly sitting down in the big porch swing, I began to fight back tears. Would I always be faced with the terror and the dark pit

I seemingly had fallen into? What future could be found in all this mess? My thoughts were interrupted when Mother came out of the outhouse and saw me sitting on the porch. Somehow, I think she knew something was wrong. I could breathe a sigh of relief as she walked to the porch and sat down in the rocking chair close to the swing.

I looked up, and Ted was peering through the screen door at me. I wanted to tell Mother what Ted had done, but fear held me back. Ted came out and sat down beside Mother, peering at me with those eyes that looked like those of the devil himself. I said not a word as I dropped my eyes, staring at my feet. Ted told mother he was thinking of going to the little country store to pick up some loaf bread for sandwiches. Mother decided to go with him as I continued to stare at my feet without saying a word.

Mother said, "Joyce, you stay here and babysit Junior." That suited me just fine! For a short period, I would escape Ted's evil eyes and hands that pawed constantly at me. My situation became worse every day, and I didn't understand what I had done to deserve this abuse. What was my alternative, and where could I receive help? *God, where are you?* was spinning through my mind continually. *Please, help me to get away from this monster.*

Ted and Mother returned home much too soon for my taste. I was lying on the sofa and Junior was sitting in the floor watching TV when the car pulled into the driveway. I hustled to get the TV turned off before they came into the house. I would sure be in trouble if Ted caught us with it on. Jumping up, I ran outside to the porch. I would yet again have to face Ted's evil eyes. Mother called for me to come and help her carry the items they had purchased. As she handed me a bag of groceries, I peered down into the bag. Ted had purchased a six-pack of beer.

Here we go again, another drinking binge. He was the meanest man I had ever known and became even worse when he was drinking. I slowly took the bag and set it on the kitchen table. Turning to walk out, I met Ted in the doorway. He pinched my bottom as I walked by! My first reaction was to draw back and slap the fire out of him. However, I knew I would pay a dear price if I attempted to go through with my impulse. I quickly moved out of reach and walked outside. My hatred for him made my temper reach the boiling point at times. I imagined waiting by the door with his old shotgun and blowing his head off when he came through. After all, he deserved nothing less than death for the pain he was inflicting on me. However, I never really had the courage to follow through with my thoughts. Making it through the day without losing my sanity was my goal.

Ted continued to make sexual gestures every chance he could. His dark and twisted mind seemed ever more determined to make my life a living hell. Every day I tried to keep my guard up to protect myself. Yet he always found a way to reach across the line with his perverted hands and mind. Somehow, I knew deep down that I would eventually escape. I did not know how long it would take nor when the door would open. But when it did, I would be ready.

CHAPTER 33

Reflection in the Mirror

 As I continued to look for ways to stay clear of Ted's abusive words and demanding hands, I stood for hours at the kitchen sink, looking at my pale refection in the mirror above it. I knew the young girl looking back at me could become something someday, if she didn't give up.

As I became a young lady, I began to take pride in keeping my face and body clean. It was a priority for me. My hair was always soft and silky-looking, even though all I had to wash with was Ivory soap. One night when I was fourteen, Ted entered the kitchen while I was washing my face. He began blasting me about using soap, having the lights on, and looking in the mirror. I truly didn't understand at the time why he would be so upset about me being in the kitchen and looking in the mirror. For me, it was an escape into a fairy tale life. As I looked in the mirror I would talk to myself, saying, *someday I will have a better life.* There were many days that would be the only thing that kept me sane.

I quickly dried my face and walked into the living room to sit down beside Mother. Relieved to be out of Ted's reach and his penetrating eyes, I looked at Mother, hoping she would come to my defense. But she said nothing. I finally asked Mother if I could go to bed.

"It's really early," she replied.

"I know, but I am tired," I said. She finally nodded her head that I could go to bed. I jumped up and almost ran to the bedroom in tears. One more night under the same roof with Ted was one night too many. However, I would make the best of a bad situation until the day came that I could leave.

The next morning it was pouring down rain. That meant I would have to face Ted at the breakfast table. He worked outside, and when it rained he stayed at home.

I planned to linger in my room and wait for the school bus to come so I wouldn't have to face his abusive mouth before leaving for school. Eventually, I heard the bus driver honking his horn. I ran into the kitchen without looking up, grabbed a biscuit, and ran out of the door. That was a relief! I didn't have to have any contact with Ted that morning.

The afternoon came, and it was time for me to return home from school. As the bus pulled up in front of the house, I didn't know what to expect because Ted had been home all day and was probably well on his way to a drinking binge. As I walked through the front door, he was sitting on the sofa. He had a smirk on his face. Walking by him without speaking, I went into the kitchen where Mother was standing. I opened one of the cabinets to find something to snack on until supper was ready. As I turned around, I observed that the mirror over the sink was missing. I looked at Mother and asked, "What happened to the mirror?"

Before she could answer, Ted yelled from the living room, "I took it down. You won't be spending hours in the kitchen looking at yourself in the mirror anymore."

I looked at Mother. She just placed her finger over her lips. I really didn't understand this man. He was crazy in my eyes. I wasn't doing anything that was hurting anyone! How would I see to fix my hair before I left for school and church? His whole plan was to make me sit where he could look at me and make obscene gestures. Ted was a pervert of the worst kind. The next time Mother went to town she found some way to purchase me a small mirror without Ted knowing. One day when she came home from the grocery store, she slipped the mirror to me when he wasn't looking. It was very small, but it was better than nothing.

Summer came, giving me the opportunity to sit out on the front porch swing to escape Ted's evil eyes and his abusive hands. Sometimes a bad thunderstorm rolled in while I was sitting on the porch. Rather than sit inside with Ted, I stayed out on the porch. I prayed that lightning would not strike the metal chains that suspended the swing from the ceiling and strike me dead! I sat until the rain began to drench my clothes. At that point I had no alternative but to go into the house. The very minute I entered the living room, Ted would start cussing at me about my wet clothes and telling me that he would not take me to the doctor if I got sick.

"You can just die. I'm not spending good money on the likes of you," he would say. Thank God I never did get sick, because he really would have let me die before he would have taken me to the doctor.

It seemed to be a never-ending cycle of verbal and sexual abuse with no end in sight. But somehow, I kept holding on to the dream of escape. There were days that it was hard to hold on to that dream. But the dream I held in my heart would be what would eventually deliver me from my abusive situation. To lose hope would have had the same effect on my life as if I were to stop breathing. I knew that I must find a way to survive and build a better life for myself somewhere else.

CHAPTER 34

Escape the Cruelty

Eventually, I met a neighbor and her daughter who lived close to the church I attended. I was walking by one Sunday after church and they started talking with me. It was a Godsend. They invited me to come for a visit. I began walking to their house often, visiting for hours to escape Ted. There were times I knew I stayed too long, but I couldn't help wanting to be somewhere safe. If Jody and her mother had only known what a blessing it was for me, they would have understood why I never wanted to go home. I dared not say anything. I had been warned of the consequences if I told anyone about what was going on behind the closed doors of our house of horror.

Jody gave me a skirt and a blouse to wear to church. I didn't have many clothes, because Mother was not allowed to buy me anything. Most of my clothes were given to me by another neighbor. I guess they saw a need and felt sorry for a teenage girl who had to wear clothes that were mostly worn out. Thank God for the compassion of neighbors.

Even through all the pain and confusion, I continued to be faithful in attending church. Eventually, the new pastor's daughter befriended me. We hit it off! Vickie invited me to her home. However, she was never allowed to come to my house. Pastor Jones visited Mother and Ted regularly. He tried very hard to get them to come to church on Sunday mornings, but they never showed up. However, Pastor Jones kept coming by. I guess he

116

hoped his persistence would pay off, but not with Ted. No way would he go back to that church.

I often wondered if Pastor Jones knew that something dreadful was going on behind closed doors at my house. Ted didn't say anything to me about spending time at Vickie's house._However, that too would change. I was excited to have three places I could go to escape Ted's cruel hands and verbal abuse: the church, Jody's house, and Vickie's house. Things seemed to be going much better for me, and I was becoming wiser about Ted's tricks.

Ted often attempted to grab me as I walked by, but I always managed to break his hold and run outside. I continued to tell Mother what he was doing, but she stayed with him. I really didn't understand how she could live with a man who was so evil! At one point when I told her what he was doing, she told me to kick him between the legs where his private parts were, and he would for sure turn me loose. I had tried it once before on our fishing trip years ago, however it hadn't worked to the degree I had hoped it would. Nevertheless I was willing to try it again and I was much stronger now.

One day Mother had walked to the neighbor's house across the street to give her some vegetables out of our garden. I was unaware she had left. Seeing a chance, as I walked through the living room to go to the porch, Ted tried to push me down on the couch. Remembering what she said, I drew back my leg and kicked him between the legs. He rolled to one side in pain. I scrambled up and ran out the front door as Ted was cussing me and calling me all kinds of names. It had worked better this time. I was free and I never slowed down. He wouldn't be bothering me for a while! I ran to the neighbor's house and sat down, out of breath. My heart was beating faster than a locomotive out of control on a downhill railroad track. Something must have shown on my face, because Mother asked me what was wrong. I told her I was okay, but from my sad eyes she knew Ted had been up to something. I didn't dare say anything in front of the neighbor, because Ted had told me about the painful consequences that would result if I did. I always thought the neighbor suspected that I was being abused, but she never said anything.

When we left the neighbor's and walked home, I told Mother what had happened. She said, "Good enough for him. He won't bother you for a while."

I still didn't understand why she wouldn't leave this evil man. When we came through the door, I could tell he was really mad. However, while

Mother was present he acted as if nothing happened. He was a good actor in every situation. I followed Mother everywhere she went that night, never letting her out of my sight. I was truly afraid Ted might follow through with his threats, and I knew the price would be great for what I did.

The price I had to pay was his refusal to let me visit my two new friends because of what I had done. I was devastated. He never stated that as the reason, but I knew too well what he was up to. Nevertheless, he did not try to keep me from attending church at that time. I guess he was afraid Pastor Jones would show up and question why I wasn't in church. He did demand I walk straight there and back. Sometimes, I stayed over after church at the pastor's house, although I knew I faced being slapped though the face for disobeying Ted's order.

On one occasion, I was at Jody's house after church when Ted's car pulled into her driveway. I looked at Jody and said, "I'm dead in the water if he finds me here."

Jody told me to run and hide in her bedroom. Ted approached the door. I could hear him talking to Jody, but could not hear clearly what they were saying. Then I heard the door close. I slowly came out of the bedroom to see what Jody had told him.

"I told Ted you were not here," she said. My friend Jody had lied to protect me! I thanked her repeatedly. I glanced out the window and saw Ted driving in the direction of the church. It was my chance to run home before Ted found out that Jody had lied about me not being at her house. I thanked Jody again and ran as fast as possible home. When Ted came around the curve, there I sat on the front porch. He pulled into the driveway and gave me a look that said I was in a bunch of trouble.

He walked up on the porch, grabbed me by the arm, and pulled me out of the swing. I started crying. It was at that point that Mother intervened. "Ted, turn her loose and leave her alone," Mother said.

He shoved me back into the swing so hard that I bounced off the back of the swing. He started cussing and called me a whore. "You won't be going anywhere for a while. You should have come straight home from church," he said.

My heart sank with the pain of having to be around him with no outlet. Many times I felt like an animal, caged with nowhere to go. I was trapped in a corner, knowing the only way out was to claw my way out of the situation that became more dangerous day after day.

However, when Ted left to drink with his buddies, I would sneak off and visit Jody for a short period. I tried to make sure I was home and sitting on the porch when he returned, but on some occasions I made it back just in time or a little late. I would walk through the woods to my neighbor's house and pretend I had been visiting her. She never told Ted, and I was grateful. I was hopeful that when I turned sixteen, one of my friends might ask me to move in. They could tell I was miserable. However, that dream would never come true.

As the days passed, I realized that Ted would never give up abuse. He took every opportunity to torment me. What was this young girl who feared for her life going to do? I couldn't tell my friends or anyone else what was really going on behind the closed doors of our house. I knew there had to be more for me than an abusive lifestyle, so I kept making plans to run away as soon as I was sixteen.

CHAPTER 35

Roadside Disaster

Six months to go! I was fifteen and a half. Weekends never changed. Sometimes on Saturday afternoons we would drive around looking for yard sales. However, it seemed we always ended up at a bar where Ted would start his binge drinking. Ted and Mother went in and stayed for hours.

Junior and I would sit in the car and just wait. The majority of the time we would fall asleep from the warm sun shining through the car window. When we woke up it would be dark out, with no sight of Mother and Ted When they finally came out of the bar, my stepfather was so drunk he couldn't stand up, let alone drive! So I climbed behind the steering wheel and drove us home. I still had no driver's license and no insurance, but I had become a very good driver. By now I had a lot of experience. Nevertheless, I was still taking a great risk in driving without a license.

One Saturday when we were in town, a policeman pulled up in front of the grocery store. Ted was standing outside at the door. The policemen approached him and said, "A report was made that someone underage has been driving your car."

"Who has reported such a thing? That's not true. Someone is trying to cause trouble," Ted said. He was a good liar, as I said before. The policeman just cautioned Ted on letting someone drive without a license and left. It must have put the fear of God in him, because he stopped letting me drive when he was over-the-top drunk. Mother tried to drive a few times, but she ran the car into a ditch, so that ended her driving.

One rainy summer day when Ted was off work, he decided it was time to take me to get my learner's permit. Of course, this was motivated by fear that we might be pulled over when he was on one of his drunken binges. He knew the police were on the outlook for me driving his car, so he figured he had better legalize my driving. Ted and Mother discussed the fact that I needed to get my permit in case I needed to drive them home.

My assumption was that everyone would be going. However, when we got up to leave, Ted told Mother there was really no reason for her to go. Fear struck my heart. My lips trembled as I said, "No. I want Mother to go with us."

Mother glanced over at me and said, "You will be fine. Anyway, I need to pick beans to can for the winter while you are gone."

"I'm not going to hurt you", Ted said.

"But Mother, I want you with me," I pleaded, with tears filling my eyes. .

She looked at me and said again, "Oh, go on, you will be fine. He is not going to hurt you."

"But Mother, you need to go," I pleaded once again. I don't know where she had been all these years, but I remembered very clearly how sneaky Ted was. A leopard didn't change its spots, and I feared the worst from him. I had tried very hard to keep out of his reach and now Mother was insisting I be alone with this monster?

"No, I'm not going if Mother doesn't go," I said.

Mother replied again, "Joyce, you need to go on and get your learner's permit. You'll be okay."

Ted said, "Come on, we need to get this over with so you can drive when we need you to."

I gave Mother a look of desperation, but it was of no use.

"Let's get this over with. I have other things I need to do," Ted said once again. I gave Mother another pleading look of desperation, but she never made a move to rescue me.

Reluctantly, I headed for the car. Not a word was said the whole time we traveled to the examining office. When we pulled up in front of the building, I jumped out as soon as he parked the car. *So far, so good,* I said to myself. Ted hadn't said anything bad to me, nor had he tried to touch me in any way. Maybe Mother had put the fear of God in him, I thought.

Whatever the reason, Ted had been a perfect gentlemen on the way to the office.

My name was called, and I approached the desk of a gentleman who seemed very kind. He handed me the test. My hands were shaking. As I took the test, I was a little nervous. My hands started sweating and shaking even more. What if I didn't pass the test? I slowly handed in my test paper and took a seat. The examiner called me to his desk again. I sat down anxiously.

"Congratulations," he said.

I looked up and replied, "Did I pass?"

"We don't usually congratulate someone who doesn't pass," he teased with a grin.

Excited to have passed the test, I asked Ted as we left the building if I could drive home.

I guess I was so excited about passing the test, I forgot what a monster he really was.

"No," he replied. "We need to get home to help your mother with the canning. Maybe later we all can take a ride and I'll let you drive then."

At the time, I didn't quite understand why he wouldn't let me drive home. After all, I had just gotten my permit, and I was a legal driver now! However, I would soon find out why Ted wanted to be the one driving home.

The way back to our house was a long two lane road with little to no traffic. Wooded lots lined the road with occasional pull-out-areas. I became a little anxious; because I knew about his history of deception. But Ted hadn't said anything out of the way on our trip, so I assumed he would keep his word about not making any abusive advances. What a mistake it was for me to trust anything he said.

All of a sudden, the car started slowing down. "What's wrong?" I asked.

"The car isn't acting right," he replied.

"What do you mean?"

"Well, it seems to be cutting out on me. I need to pull over somewhere and check it out," he replied. He slowly pulled over onto the roadside, but continued to drive off into the woods.

"What are you doing? You don't need to pull back into the woods," I responded with fear in my heart. I grabbed for the door handle just as he grabbed for my arm. He pulled me back and locked the door as the car came to a stop.

"Why are you pulling back in the woods?" I asked. He never replied. What was I to do now? Once again I had trusted Ted, and once again he had betrayed me. I started sobbing.

"Shut up and take your medicine," he said with a grin. As he pushed me down in the seat. I was screaming and kicking with all my might. However, no matter how much I screamed, no one heard me! It seemed to excite him even more as I tried to push him away. I will never forget the pain, the humiliation, and the fear I felt that day. It brought back the memory of how he had tried to kill me years earlier. What else would he do to me? I pushed with all my might, trying desperately to get him off me! Then I must have blacked out. When I opened my eyes, he was bent over me and shaking me with all his might. He must have thought I was dead. He pushed me back onto the seat, shut the door, and locked it.

I pulled myself up as much as possible with tear-filled eyes and fear in my heart. In my opinion, my life was a festered wound ready to burst open from all the pain I had endured. How could I have been so stupid as to have trusted this evil man? How could Mother insist I come with him, knowing how abusive he had been in the past? I hated Mother for making me go with him alone. She must have known he was up to something when he encouraged her to stay at home.

He stood outside, looking at me through the window. What was he up to now? "You stay in the car," he said.

He had locked both doors, and the windows were up. I became even more afraid of what he might do. He walked around in front of the car to the driver's side. He opened the door, got back in the car, and started it without saying a word. As the car moved through the thick wooded area onto the highway, my hand touched the door handle. He looked over and grabbed my arm.

"Get your hand off that door handle," he said. I slowly moved my hand away and slumped down in the seat, feeling shame and humiliation yet again. On the way home, I had nothing to say. I just continued to cry and look out the window. Right before we reached the house, he spoke up.

"You had better keep your mouth shut and dry up those alligator tears," he said. We pulled up into the driveway. I was slow to get out of the car. Mother came outside on the porch to see if I had passed the test.

Before I could say anything, Ted spoke up. "She passed, and now she can drive without fear of being stopped. How many beans have you picked?"

I turned to go in the house, but was stopped by Mother, who asked me to help her with the rest of the beans. I sat down in a chair on the porch and started breaking beans. I didn't have a lot to say, because I was still shaking from the ordeal that had happened on our way back. As soon as we finished the beans, I entered the house and went straight to my bedroom. I cried myself to sleep.

When Mother called me for supper, I told her I wasn't feeling well and was not hungry. Thank God, she believed me. I didn't sleep very well the rest of that night, because I kept thinking about how stupid I had been to go with this evil man. I mentally rehearsed what I should have done to get away. I felt shame and guilt for letting myself get into another situation where he could abuse me. I knew I must work harder to find a way out of this hell on earth. I was determined never to be alone with him again.

A few weeks after that horrible afternoon, Ted's mother Sally came for a visit. She stayed for an extended period. That was the greatest gift I could receive, because Sally would be sleeping in my room. That meant I slept in peace, without worrying about him coming into my room. Sally was a sweet woman, and I wondered many times how she had such an evil son. Many times I wanted to tell her what was going on behind closed doors, but fear held me back from any conversation about the whole issue. Ted was a different person when Sally was around! He put up a good front in her presence. He had her fooled just like the rest. However, I knew he was a wolf in sheep's clothing.

Her leaving came much too soon for me. I avoided him at all costs. However, the very minute she left the house, the verbal abuse and the grabbing of my clothes would start right back where they had left off when she came for her visit. Those few months of peace had given me the courage to work harder to be free from the clutches of his hands. *I will be free,* I repeated daily.

CHAPTER 36

In the Nick of Time

The day finally came when I turned sixteen. I persuaded Mother to allow me to work at a small restaurant in town. That was the beginning of my escape. I made twenty-five dollars a week, good money for a little country girl who had nothing. Ted took part of the money for rent. I usually took a taxi home from work, so I didn't have a lot left, but I saved what few dollars I could faithfully. Sometimes Mother and Ted would pick me up after work, especially on payday. Ted wanted to make sure he got his rent money first.

I let Mother know from the beginning that if Ted came by himself, I would not get in the car with him. He never showed up without her, so I was never confronted with the issue. There were a few times that I walked home because I didn't have money for a taxi. It was a long walk, but I didn't care. I spent most of it encouraging myself to escape that house and never look back! I worked hard for long hours, moving toward the light at the end of the tunnel. I put back as much as possible toward a brighter future. The verbally abusive circumstances had come to seem almost normal. It is amazing how you can adapt to things in order to keep your sanity.

Day after day, I made plans and put them into action. The owners of the restaurant told me about a lady who rented out rooms in town. It would help me save more money if I rented a room rather than give most of what I made to Ted, and I wouldn't have to pay for taxis either. I took an afternoon off to look at the room. It was small, and I would have to share the bathroom with other tenants. However, I would at least have peace in my life for the first time, and would be able to sleep without fear. That was enough incentive to offset how small it was. Anything was a step above living with Ted.

I made a down payment to the landlady, promising to give her the remainder on Friday. I was so excited I could hardly contain myself. I had to remember to not show too much emotion, or Ted would become suspicious and find out my plans. If he did, he would surely try to prevent me from leaving.

That was the longest week of my life. I visited the room on Monday and planned to move my few belongings on Friday while Ted was at work. I prayed it wouldn't rain and keep him home that day.

Friday finally arrived. Early in the afternoon, I took a taxi home to get my belongings. When we pulled up in the driveway, Mother came to the door. She knew I was up to something. I was never home at that time of day.

When I opened the car door, she called out to me, "Joyce, what is going on? Why are you here at this time of day?"

I looked squarely at her as I pushed through the door and said, "Mother, I have come to get my belongings. I am leaving. I can't stand any more of the abuse."

She never tried to stop me. I gathered all of my clothes and personal items and put them in the taxi. I knew I must hurry, because Ted would be coming home from work soon. After I finished the last load, I walked back to the front porch. I looked at Mother in disbelief. Her eyes were filled with tears. Why was she crying now? She should have done something a long time ago.

"Mother, I am sorry, but I must go for my own safety. I never know what that crazy man is going to do next. You can tell him for me that if he tries to come after me, I will go to the police and tell them everything he has done. He had better stay away from me," I said.

"I will tell him," she replied. She turned to hug me, and I pulled away. I didn't want her to hug me. At that time I never wanted to see her again, either. She had let Ted abuse me for so long that in my eyes, she was as guilty as he was. I didn't care that she was crying. I turned and walked in the direction of the car. I glanced back over my shoulder as I got back into the taxi. When I sat down in the seat, I felt relief that my ordeal was almost over. But we needed to hurry, because it was getting close to the time for Ted to return from work. The taxi backed out of the driveway, and I rolled down the window. As we pulled away, I waved good-bye to Mother. She waved back with tear-filled eyes. I was delighted to be on the road to freedom. Although I was anxious about the unknown journey ahead of me, I knew anything had to be better than what I had endured for so many years!

As we rounded the curve above the house, we met Ted coming home from work. I looked back through the rear window at his taillights.

"I hate you!" came out of my mouth. The taxi driver didn't say a word, just kept on driving. We had left in the nick of time. "Thank God," I said under my breath as we drove away into a new beginning. This little country girl was relieved and happy to be free at last from the abuse of a monster. However, was I truly free?

CHAPTER 37

Heartbreak Tonight

It would take years for the healing process to complete its work in me, because the scars of my years of abuse were so deeply rooted and painful. I found out very soon how the deep root of bitterness would eat me alive in every relationship, especially when it came to men. My heart was so scarred that I became what some would call a man-hater. Determined never to let another man abuse me as Ted had, I became hard-shelled and defensive. My determination that everyone, especially men, should pay for the abuse I had suffered as a child and young lady became a driving force in my life. The opinion I had of men was very low. I felt like they all were perverted pigs who used others for their own self-gratification with no regard or consideration for boundaries.

I took a good look at the journey ahead to see if it would offer me any encouragement. But the bitterness that lay within me would undermine any chance of having a meaningful relationship with any man who dared to enter my circle of distrust, suspicion, and hatred. My attitude was a walking time bomb, waiting to explode on any man who dared to touch me sexually. Confused about the whole mess, I was left empty, angry, bitter, and running over with unforgiving resentment.

The poison of abuse that had been dished out at the hands of Ted set me on a path of self-destruction. I seemed to have lost my passion for life, and depression set in. Somehow I couldn't shake my insecurities or sense of humiliation, and those negative feelings eventually drove me away from my church roots. There was no room for God when the hatred of past pain was so fresh in my mind.

However, I would jump from the frying pan into the fire, as the old saying goes! My life took a deeper nose dive as I started running with the wrong crowd. I met Bernice through a mutual friend. She was much older than me: she had a child and was going through a divorce. I moved in with her, which was another mistake. She was as bitter as I was, because of the treatment she had received from her ex-husband. We were two people looking for love in all the wrong places.

Bernice and I would party and dance all night. I never drank alcohol, both because I simply did not like the taste and because drinking seemed completely unappealing after living with an abusive alcoholic. However, I did like dancing and having fun. I became addicted to the night life, dancing until the wee hours of the morning. Although I enjoyed it, this lifestyle came to deepen my hatred and resentment of any men who reached out to me. Whenever they reached out, I pushed them back. I didn't mind dancing with them, but that was as far as I wanted to go. As far as I was concerned, my life was tainted forever by the abuse I had suffered at the hands of others. The new life I was searching for seemed impossibly far away. Who would want me if they knew what had happened to me before? I was so ashamed of my past that I wasn't willing to share any details of it with anyone, not even family members.

I went from relationship to relationship, looking for love in all the wrong places. I never allowed anyone to get close enough to penetrate my heart and life. If any man told me he loved me, you had better believe there would be heartbreak tonight because I would run, baby, run in the other direction. I could not trust men. In my mind, they only wanted one thing, and I wasn't willing to give into a sexually relationship.

Feelings of failure and hopelessness and thoughts of suicide invaded my mind night and day. The tormenting memories were destroying any chance of a normal lifestyle. I wanted to choke Ted until the very life left his body.

I often said that Ted deserved nothing less than a tormented life of hell. I hoped I could see him burning in hell for the things he did to me. It wasn't until many years later that I understood that to see him in hell, I would have to be there too! Once I realized that, it didn't take me long to change that attitude. I'd had enough hell and disappointments to last me a lifetime, and I didn't need any more. The abuse caused me to lose sight of the things that were truly important in my life. I wanted to give up and cave in to a hopeless life of hurt. It was difficult for me to dream of a happy life while I was surrounded by a gray cloud of unforgiving bitterness. I told myself I had the right to feel as I did. I resisted any idea of forgiving someone who had inflicted so much pain on a young, innocent girl. However, I soon came to learn that forgiveness was the only way to recovery.

CHAPTER 38

120 Miles per Hour in
the Wrong Direction

Eventually, I moved in with my sister Deborah. She patiently tried to guide me in the right direction. However, I resisted her advice. I insisted that I was my own boss now and would make my own decisions. Deborah still loved me through it all.

At first, I would not visit Mother because she still lived with the monster that inflicted pure hell on my life. I wasn't ready to forgive her for the rejection she had inflicted throughout my childhood, and I surely wasn't going to forgive the man who did not deserve in my opinion to have a peaceful nights sleep. Nevertheless, the day came when God tugged at my heart where my Mother was concerned. I guess no matter how bad things are, or how old you are, you always desire a relationship with your mother! Still, I was not willing to give Ted the time of day. My visits would occur while he was at work. I was not willing to face that monster and take any chance he would try to pick up where he had left off when his abuse was still as fresh in my mind as though it had happened just yesterday.

My desire was to see him in hell and for him to be tortured for the rest of his life. I knew if I had anything to do with it, I would ensure it came to pass. He didn't deserve to be forgiven nor did he deserve to live on this earth. I couldn't stand the fact that good people were dying every day, yet God was letting him continue to live his life as if nothing had happened.

I didn't fully understand why God would let Ted continue to live after he had destroyed my life as a young girl. I often wondered how many other young girls had suffered at his hands. My visions of him dying a slow, painful death brought me great pleasure. Satisfaction would only come when the vision became reality and I could at last sigh with the relief of knowing he had finally paid for his actions.

Hard-hearted and hard-headed, I was determined that no one would ever get the opportunity to hurt me again. My heart was calloused, and the walls of protection were evident to all who attempted to build any type of relationship with me. I was determined to have a bright future, and no one had better get in my way. Just like a speeding train, I would run right over you if you dared to block the path I was determined to take.

I was strong-minded and determined that someday I would be someone. That force continuously burned in my soul like a blazing forest fire. My temper was as hot as a noon day sun on a July day. If you didn't like me or what I was doing, I could have cared less! I thought my hard shell and hot temper would protect me from anyone taking advantage of me again.

I realize now that I was losing sight of the important matters and driving my life as if it were a bulldozer plowing down every tree in the forest. Nevertheless, at that point my mental resources were in survival mode. My hard-core attitude would give me the ability to stand toe-to-toe with any man and fight him blow-for-blow if that was what it took to protect myself. There were a few times I got my tail whipped, but I still got up for more. I had more guts than intelligence, as the old saying goes. Deep in my mind, the scarred roots of bitterness drove me like a madwoman, determined that no one would take advantage of me—ever.

My determination to work harder than anyone else and finish my work in half the time of my co-workers worked against me in some ways. It made it difficult to build any type of working relationship, because my co-workers were jealous and disliked me for forcing them to work more quickly. I made every effort to shine like a diamond in the rough to get what I needed to survive. I was running a race. However, it seemed I was my only competition. Had I let my attitude get out of control? I began to stop and ask myself that question.

Nevertheless, for a long time I cared little about what people thought or how much they were hurting. I was too busy licking my own wounds. Anyway, I figured no one had been hurt any more than I had, so I really didn't care about the feelings of others. My life was a broken piece of pottery lying in the potter's field; unattractive, gray, and lifeless. Yet my bullheaded attitude drove me deeper into a life of torment. I knew something was missing. I felt empty, and the void grew deeper each day. Self-destruction became a lifestyle with no end in sight. Thoughts of suicide would invade my life once again. Why live when you were being tormented every day by demons of past pains? I was running 120 miles per hour in the wrong direction, seeking peace and never finding any. Would the demons of my past chase me to my grave?

CHAPTER 39

Reconnect

A few years later I would finally let someone penetrate my heart enough to get married, however, I had gotten married for all the wrong reason and that marriage would fail. I began to face the fact that I was destroying my own life through a vindictive lifestyle. I reconnected with my Christian roots and began attending a local church. I had tried everything else, it seemed, and nothing really gave me the peace I was so desperately searching for. Returning to church was one of my wisest decisions. It was a lifeline to a brighter future. I continued to attend church while searching daily for answers that would set me free from my life of torment. Each time the pastor made an altar call, I found myself kneeling with my face buried in my hands and a flood of tears running to the floor. It seemed that each time I got up, my load was a little lighter. As men chip at a big rock to make gravel, God continued to chip away at my heavy load of pain, rejection, and a hard-shelled attitude. However, there always seemed to be something I could not turn loose. I knew I must release the hurt and pain because forgiveness was an essential part of my recovery process. How would I ever do this with all the memories of abuse looming beneath the surface? At any moment, they could explode like a volcano whose hot running lava overflows and runs down a mountain, destroying everything in its path.

That image was burning deep in my mind because it had happened many times before. I would just lose it one day because someone pushed the wrong button. Many times I was so mad I could not remember what I had done or what I had said. I needed to get my temper under control, because when I reached the boiling point, I became so mad I could have killed someone and walked away never thinking about it twice. That frightened me. Had I let past fears and hurts cloud my very thinking? Each time I thought I was making progress, I would find more unforgiving poison bottled up. I was a walking poison machine that spat out venom like a copperhead snake. Had my life become so tormented that I had lost all hope of freedom from pain? Could I ever find the grace to forgive?

The Bible had taught me that true forgiveness and peace would only come when I was willing to forgive the ones who had abused me. Nonetheless, the pain was still fresh in my mind. It had penetrated deep into resentment within my soul. I replayed Ted's actions as if on a video screen in my mind. Shadows of abuse seemed to lurk around each corner. Would I spend my life continuing to repent for those feelings that kept me awake at night? No matter where I traveled or with whom I spent time, those feelings always hovered over me like a ghost in a haunted house. There was no rest for this country girl, and no escape from my memories of days and nights of abuse.

Even going to church didn't help me completely move past my hurt and pain. It seemed I became more suspicious of those who continued to try to build relationships with me. What did they really want? I wondered.. Pain and hurt can make you build high walls of protection around your heart and soul. The walls I built were tall and wide. Having any type of meaningful relationship was definitely out of the question. Would I ever have a normal life, or would the memories forever haunt me? Could I forgive? Would I start acting like it never happened? Where did I go from here? Was this church thing going to work in my case?

CHAPTER 40

Burn, Baby, Burn

One cold winter day, I received a call from Mother. Her words caught me by surprise. She told me that she and Ted had rededicated their lives to God and were attending church. Maybe Mother had, I thought, but Ted had done too much to be able to get off that easily! No way had he got religion. I was sure it was just an act to cover up the bad things he did. I wasn't willing to forgive this evil man for all the abuse he had put me through. Not in his lifetime. Ted could die and burn in hell as far as I was concerned. In my opinion, that would be too good for him.

Obviously, I was still bitter and hard as nails, unable to feel forgiveness for Ted. He would never be a part of my life again, I vowed, with or without religion. That was my decision, and I would stick by it. I had tried to lay it down, but the memories kept me in defense mode. He was a devil in human skin, in my opinion, and he deserved nothing less than unbearable torture. Religion, my foot! He didn't have religion; he was just trying to get a quick fix on a fire escape to bypass hell. I wanted him to burn, baby, burn for his evil deeds. No heaven for him! Only when you could find snowballs in hell would I believe that Ted had changed.

Nevertheless, Ted and Mother continued to attend church. Still, I wasn't convinced it was real. Ted needed to prove a lot before I would ever believe he had found religion. I sat back and watched from the sidelines with doubt and disbelief. It would not last this time any more than it had lasted before, I figured. He was a devil in sheep's clothing, and I waited for him to fall flat on his ugly face. I could see right through all his phony and superficial religion. Religion was more than going to church and going through the motions. I would believe his story when hell froze over, and not before.

But yet again, I felt the hands of God tugging at my heart to forgive. I chose to ignore God and this whole forgiveness thing. I always made one more excuse why I should not forgive those who had hurt me. They needed to ask me for forgiveness, in my opinion! After all, I was the one who had suffered at their unmerciful hands of torment.

If only I had known many years ago how true forgiveness would set me free from the chains of a prisoner's life, how I would have run to God's loving arms of forgiveness and broken all the chains that had me bound in a dark dungeon of hurt and pain. I could have truly been set free by His promises and His love. However, I still hated Ted with a passion that burned like a forest fire out of control. I wasn't willing, nor was I ready, to forgive him. All that religion bull crap was just that: bull crap!

CHAPTER 41

A Call of Desperation

The phone rang. On the other end was my mother's voice.

"Hello, Joyce. I am in the hospital with Ted," Mother said. "A neighbor called the ambulance because he became disoriented and then lost consciousness. All evidence is pointing to a stroke. Ted isn't talking and isn't eating enough to keep his strength up,"

Needless to say, I wasn't very interested in what she had to say about Ted's condition. He could die for all I cared.

"Joyce, I have been here for three days and he seems worse today," she said. She sounded desperate. But what did this have to do with me? I really didn't care that he had a stroke, could not talk well, or would not eat. So what? He deserved everything he was receiving. Finally, my revenge! I must say, it felt mighty good!

She began to cry. "Joyce, can you come and help me take care of him?"

What? She must be out of her mind!

She continued, "I don't have a way back and forth from home to the hospital, and I can't get him to eat."

"Who cares?" I whispered. "He can die as far as I am concerned. I really don't care what happens to him."

She had to be kidding. She was out of her ever-loving mind if she thought I was going to come and play nursemaid to the man who abused

138

me. I continued to listen with astonishment and reservation. There was no way I was going to help the man who had destroyed my young life. No way! He had caused me too much pain and suffering. Mother needed to find someone else to help her. This girl was out of Ted's presence, and she was going to stay out.

My thoughts were interrupted by her plea once again. "Joyce, please come," she said. I froze, saying nothing. "Are you there?" she asked.

"Yes," I answered.

"Will you come?" cried her pleading voice.

"Mother, I'm not sure I can come," I said.

"I know it is hard, but I need you," she replied.

I was choking back tears by this time. I really didn't understand why she felt I should be the one to help. Finally, I replied, "I will call you tomorrow and let you know, because I have other obligations."

I couldn't believe that came out of my mouth! I didn't have any intention of going, and I didn't know why I had said that. I imagine I said it to just get off the phone.

"Okay, I look forward to hearing from you tomorrow. Please make every effort to come," she said. The phone clicked on the other end as I slowly placed the receiver back on the base. Why had she called me? I couldn't do this. She was asking too much from a girl who had suffered so much pain at the hands of a monster.

I slowly walked outside and sat down on the porch. That seemed to be the place I always retreated to when things were tough. I tried to convince myself that I had every right to refuse to help Ted. God doesn't expect me to help, I thought. Why did Mother think she had the right to request that I come and help? I searched my Bible for a way out, but everything I turned to was saying, "I have forgiven you, and you must forgive him."

Forgive him! No way would I do that! That was too much to ask. After a few hours, I went to bed. However, sleep did not come. I still heard Mother's pleading voice. Finally, after tossing and turning most of the night, I decided to get up. I went to the closet, pulled out some clothing, and started packing a suitcase. What was I doing? Shocked, I paused and turned to go back to bed, but something kept tugging me to go. Why? I went to the bathroom to get my toothbrush. Placing it in my suitcase, I paused again in hesitation. I wasn't sure if I should go. However, it seemed I was being controlled by my feet. I found myself standing in front of the car. I opened the car door and begin loading my suitcase. It was around four o'clock in the morning. It would take about two and a half hours to reach the hospital. Why was I leaving now? I wondered. Could I not wait until daybreak? I knew in my heart that I could not, though I couldn't say why.

As soon as I pulled out of my driveway, I began to pray and seek God's direction. I prayed awhile, cried awhile, and told myself I was crazy for going. It was a long, lonely drive on a dark road of pain. As I was driving, I once again felt the pain that I had suffered at Ted's hands. Why was I going to help a man who didn't deserve my help?

CHAPTER 42

Run, Baby, Run

As I pulled up into the hospital parking lot, daylight began to break. The sun peeked over the distant mountain. I bowed my head to pray. "God, please help me. I can't do this unless you help. I am not strong enough to face this man". As I looked up, the sun was shining on my windshield. Its reflection was almost blinding to my eyes. I sat there for a few minutes in silence. Could I really follow through with this?

Finally, I opened the car door and started walking to the front door of the hospital. Many questions nagged at my consciousness as I walked through the entrance. My legs seemed heavy and limp at the same time. As I entered the elevator, I paused, thinking of turning around and running back to the car. However, my legs directed me onward.

"Oh God, I can't do this," I said to myself once again. The elevator ride was much too short for my liking. The door opened and I stood there, feet glued to the floor. I had to push the button again, because the door was closing. Finally, I slowly stepped out of the elevator into the hall that led to Ted's room. As I turned to walk down what seemed to be a mile-long hallway, I paused to get my emotions under control. The aching wounds from years of abuse were present again. Standing there, the thought of running back to my car entered my mind once again. No one would ever know I had been here. Now was my chance to forget the whole thing and go back home. Nevertheless, something seemed to be pulling me down the hall. I felt myself resisting, but the more I held back, the closer I came to the door.

Suddenly, there I was, standing in front of the door. What would I do now? Run, baby, run was my first thought. It still wasn't too late! My legs moved me slowly through the door. Each one felt like it weighted fifty pounds. Mother turned and saw me standing in the doorway. Too late to leave now!

She smiled and said, "I am so glad you are here."

I nodded my head and moved forward slowly. Here lay the man I hated so much, frail and motionless. Ted opened his eyes. I drew back, afraid of what he would say. However, to my surprise, he raised his hand in a gesture for me to come over to his bed. *No*, I thought in the back of my mind, *I can't do this*. Still, I felt my feet moving forward. Ted couldn't speak well because of the stroke, so he said not a word. However, he seemed different. I didn't know what it was, and truthfully I didn't care.

Mother came to my side and hugged me. I was stiff as a board and very unimpressed. I pulled away from her passionate show of thankfulness that I had come. I didn't want her hugs, nor did I really care how she felt. The only time it seemed she had any compassion for me was when she needed something. I was in no mood for her superficial caring.

She began to repeat what happened. I wasn't really interested, but I pretended to listen. My mind raced ninety miles an hour. My face flushed with hatred for Ted. He deserved to die, I thought.

We were interrupted by a nurse bringing his breakfast tray. I stepped back, relieved for the opportunity to stop looking at Ted's disgusting face. The nurse left the room as quickly as she had entered. This left Mother and me standing there in silence. Mother stepped forward to help Ted with his breakfast. Her face was that of a tired, old lady. The lines in her face seemed much deeper than the last time I saw her. Yet she continued to push herself past her ability, to care for the man who had given her nothing but a life of living hell. Why had she stayed in that abusive situation? God and she were the only ones who knew the answer to that question.

Signs of weakness were evident in Ted's frail, broken body. He hadn't eaten enough in days to keep up his strength. However, I really didn't care how weak, sick, or frail he was. Suddenly, Mother turned to me and said, "Joyce, will you try to get Ted to eat something?"

I stared back at her with unbelieving eyes. Help him eat something? I wanted to shove a spoon down his throat until he choked. I may have rededicated my life to God, but I still didn't like him, nor did I think he deserved to live!

She turned to me again and said, "Are you going to help me?"

I stood there, still as if I had a ball and chain on my feet. I began to shake and felt a little light-headed. My face was burning as if it was on fire. How could she ask me to do this? Feed the man who had inflicted so much pain into a little girl's life? He deserved nothing short of slow torture and then death. I felt the bitterness and rage welling up. *How could I make it look like an accident?* I thought while I stood there, weak and trembling.

Mother turned again and asked for the third time, "Well, are you going to help or not?"

"Can't you do it?" were the words I heard leaving my mouth.

"Joyce, I am tired, and I need your help," she pleaded. By this time, without realizing it, I had backed all the way into the doorway of the room. Should I step outside into the hallway and get my emotions under control, or should I step forward and help?

I remember uttering a prayer under my breath. "Oh God, please help me. I can't do this unless you give me the grace to follow through." Before I knew what had happened, I was at Ted's bedside. I reached for the spoon on his tray and slowly spooned out a small amount of food. My hand shook and I felt beads of perspiration on my forehead. I felt sick to my stomach. Could I actually do this? As I moved the spoon to Ted's mouth, our eyes met. I froze with fear. Should I run at this point and forget the whole thing? Shaking and fearful, I stood with a raised spoon in hand and eyes filled with hatred.

Before me, instead of the evil eyes of the abusive man I remembered, there were eyes filled with pain, suffering and sadness. Maybe he really did rededicate his life to God? I lifted the spoon to his mouth, but he gave little response. Then, without any foreknowledge or self-will, my mouth opened and out spilled, "You must eat, or you are not going to make it out of this hospital."

He glanced up, opened his mouth, and took the spoon filled with food. Not another word was said, but he did eat most of his food. Now, I saw for the first time a humble, repenting man lying at death's door. We never exchanged words on that day or any other, but somehow his eyes reflected his regret and sadness for the deeds of cruelty he had inflicted on my life. Still, reservations and distrust lingered in my heart. Ted had always been a good actor. He had done it many times before. Why should this one be any different?

As Mother and I left the hospital that day, I said little. God had been dealing with my heart, and I didn't like it one bit! I had a right to feel hatred for Ted—even if he was sick and at death's door. I had fed him, and in my mind, that was my way of forgiving him. However, deep down inside I felt revenge lurking beneath the surface of the hard shell I portrayed. I enjoyed knowing it was time for him to pay. When I drove Mother back to her house, I was relieved as we rounded the curve and I saw my brother's car in the driveway. That meant I could go home tonight.

CHAPTER 43

Long Road Back Home

With my goodbyes said, I turned to my car and headed up the road for the two-and-a-half-hour drive that was ahead of me. I was tired and anxious to get out of that town, away from all the reminders of events that penetrated my childhood.

"This is a town I will never live in again," I said under my breath. Too many bad memories of yesterday's pains lingered in my mind and thoughts. My desire to pick up the pieces and move on to a peaceful life was as strong as a craving for a cold drink of water on a hot summer day. I craved the peace of a better life and would pursue it at all costs. However, that day brought back all my old feelings and hurts. It wasn't fair, and I didn't think I should have to endure any more pain and heartache because of the past events that had robbed me of my childhood.

"Why me, Lord?" was always on my lips. What had I done that would require me to endure a life of pain? Of course, at the time I didn't realize that God was trying to help me get past the pain and into a healing process that would bring rebirth to my life and my relationships. All my relationships had crumbled apart, because I did not trust people, especially men'. Piece by piece, like a puzzle being put together, God began a process of repair in my life. Nonetheless, I remained reluctant to believe this horrible man had changed! On the drive home, I couldn't stop thinking about the ordeal of that day. The pressure of the day was more than any human should have to bear, I thought. I thought all of this was behind me. I knew the road of life had many detours, but this was one I didn't want to take! I had done nothing wrong, in my eyes, so why was I the one who had to forgive? I was the innocent child, the victim. He should be pleading with me to forgive him! Yet the words that filled my heart were, "If you want me to forgive you, then you must truly forgive him."

It was like a wrestling match in my mind. God said one thing, and I responded with a reason why I kept those feelings bottled up inside. The great thing about God is that He knows our heart and soul. He is the one person we cannot fool, even when we try! However, that didn't stop me. I still made excuses of why I felt the way I did. Still, God did not give up on me, and today I am so glad He didn't! He had a plan for me, and that plan would never materialize if I didn't release the whole situation into His hands. He was the healer, and His healing would stick if I would do my part and release the hurt and pain. God continued to work on my heart as I drove further away from the hell I once lived. I cried a river of tears, screamed, and yelled at God.

Then suddenly I screamed out loud. "Okay, God. Help me to truly forgive him completely. But you know I can't do this unless you walk me through this forgiving grace and mercy."

The twenty-third Psalm came to my mind. "Yea, though I walk through the valley of the shadow of death, I will fear no evil; for You are with me; Your rod and Your staff, they comfort me." I needed comfort from God. I felt I was walking through the valley of the shadow of death, and everywhere I went I had a big rain cloud over my head. The death I would experience in my life was more of a rebirth, a renewal of life. It was taking off an old mindset and stony heart and replacing them with a new mindset and a heart transplanted by God! Ezekiel 11:19 says, "I will put a new spirit within them, and take the stony heart out of their flesh." (NKJV)

The process continued for many years. At least I moved forward, with God's helping hand. Some people say it happens all at once, but for me it was a process, little by little. Maybe God knew I couldn't deal with it all at once. Whatever the reason, it was like peeling an onion off my life, one layer at a time. I never really understood everything, but I trusted that God would bring me through to the other side with a healed mind, body, and soul. I knew the baggage I carried was too heavy a load and I had to let it go, yet deep inside I still felt I was holding back on God.

CHAPTER 44

Death Came

Ted was released from the hospital. However, he never fully recovered. He had a blood clot in his brain. Doctors said he was a walking time bomb that could explode at any time. Any time came one fall afternoon. He walked outside and never returned. About twenty minutes after he left, Mother found him in the outhouse, slumped over and dead. That morning he had complained of a headache. Mercifully, God spared Mother from seeing him draw his last breath. I really think Ted also knew his time had arrived and walked outside to spare Mother the pain of watching him die right in front of her eyes.

The call came while I was cooking dinner. "Hello," I said.

The voice on the other end was crying. I realized it was Mother.

"What is wrong?" I asked.

"He's dead," she replied.

"Who?"

"Ted."

Just for a second, I felt satisfaction. Finally, he was gone. I realized I was not yet finished with the process of forgiveness.

I was drawn back to the call by the plea in Mother's voice. "Can you come and help me with his funeral arrangements?"

What? I had helped when he was in the hospital, and now she wanted me to help with the funeral arrangements? No way. It was someone else's turn! As far as I was concerned, my job was done.

"Joyce, will you come?" Mother repeated.

Something inside me did not let me refuse her request. However, had I known about the layer of unforgiveness that would be peeled off that day, I would have probably stayed home. Sometimes it is good that the blueprint of our lives is not laid out before we take the next step. We would never take that step if we knew all the details. Nonetheless, God in His wisdom knew what it would take to set me free at last!

Driving alone the two and a half hours to Mother's house gave me time to pray and ask God for the courage to once again face the situation with His love, mercy, and grace. It was dark when I reached the house. Mother met me at the front door. She embraced me as I entered the house, but I was still a little reluctant to show any emotion where she was concerned. Tears filled her eyes as she began to explain what needed to be done.

"Can you stay and help me?" was her request.

"I can't stay in this house! Too many horrible memories still linger in my mind about the times spent in this house," I replied. Pushing past her without another word, I went into the kitchen where others were standing. I surely didn't want to get into another conversation with her about staying, so I avoided her at all costs. Yes, I had somewhat forgiven him, but to stay here was a different issue.

People began to leave. As I looked around, I panicked, knowing she needed an answer soon. I began to pray under my breath, "Please, someone, please volunteer to stay. I just can't do this."

Fear filled my heart as I faced the fact that it would probably fall on me to stay and be in this house overnight. By this time my grandparents had passed away, so staying with them was not an option. Anyway, Mother didn't want to leave the house. She was afraid someone would break in and steal her belongings. My brother had not yet arrived; he would be there the next day. As people continued to leave, she confronted me again. "Joyce, you are going to stay with me tonight, aren't you?"

I finally gave in to her request. I was not a happy camper about being placed in that dilemma, but what was I to do?

With the departure of all the visitors and family, Mother and I sat on the sofa until the wee hours of the morning talking. I just couldn't face staying in my old bedroom, so I told Mother to go to bed, and I would rest on the sofa. I don't remember getting much sleep, if any, that night.

But I did what I needed to do to help Mother with the pain of losing her husband. The pain of knowing she never was there for me when I needed her crept into my mind. I felt resentment welling up in my heart, but I knew I must push that aside and do what I had to do to help Mother, no matter what happened in the past.

Morning didn't arrive soon enough for me. I was ready to get the whole thing over with. I drove Mother to the funeral home to make arrangements. The drive took about thirty minutes, which gave us enough time to discuss how much she could spend. I convinced Mother that she must stay within her budget. She would need finances for her living expenses. She agreed, and we were set to tell the funeral home director the amount to be spent and still have a nice funeral. As we arrived, one of Ted's brothers met us at the front door. The first thing out of Bob's mouth was, "Ted will have a nice funeral, if I have to pay for it myself."

I looked at him in disbelief. Why did he say such a thing? Mother had every intention of doing a nice funeral. However, had I known what would be placed on my shoulders yet again, I would have run in the opposite direction and let Bob take care of the whole funeral and all the expenses.

When we entered the funeral home, we were greeted by the funeral home director. He was very polite and comforting to Mother. There was no insurance to pay for Ted's funeral, so that meant no money to pay for his funeral expenses. The only money Mother could count on was the two hundred and fifty dollars that social security paid and the social security benefits she would receive as his wife. What would Mother do? She had nothing except the house, a few household items, and the clothes in her closet. Bob was of no help other than trying to tell Mother what suit and casket to purchase. Bob said he would take care of the costs if he needed to. That big talk disappeared when the director asked how the funeral was to be paid. Not a single word came out of Bob's mouth then. I thought to myself, *Talk is cheap, buddy. Back up those words with actions.* But the room remained silent while Bob looked at the floor to avoid eye contact with us or the funeral home director.

Mother glanced over at me. I sat there in disbelief. What was she looking at me for? The words that came out of her mouth shocked me. Mother said, "Joyce, can you help me pay for the funeral?"

I shook my head while my eyes filled with tears. She actually expected me to help pay for the funeral of a man who repeatedly abused me? What more would be asked of me? Still Bob never spoke up about helping with the expenses. I couldn't believe Mother would have the guts to ask me to help pay for Ted's funeral. Besides, I didn't have that kind of money. I lived from paycheck to paycheck, just like everyone else. I guess she thought I just pick money off the trees in my front yard each time a need arose. At least that was the impression I got from her request.

I looked at Mother with eyes of disbelief and said, "No, Mother, I can't. I don't have that kind of money just lying around."

The funeral home director interrupted our conversation. "Will you sign a legally binding contract stating that one of you will pay?"

Mother looked at me again. I wasn't signing a contract! I replied to the funeral home director's request, "The only thing she has is the house. As soon as we can sell it, I will make sure you are paid."

Still not a word from Bob lips. Silence filled the room for what seemed ten minutes. However, only a few seconds passed. The director must have heard the desperation in my voice and seen it on my face. He glanced over at Bob, who was still staring at the floor. Evidently the funeral home director knew he wasn't going to be helped by Bob's actions, so he said, "I tell you what I'm going to do. If your Mother will sign this contract that she will pay when the house sells, I will do the funeral."

We agreed, and I felt slightly relieved. I thanked God for opening the heart of a generous man. Because of his generosity, when the house eventually sold, he was the first one to receive payment in full.

The director turned to Mother and said, "Are you ready to go pick out his suit and casket?"

"Oh no, Joyce will have to do that," Mother said.

My mouth dropped open in disbelief. "Me! No way, Mother. That is your duty," I replied.

"But, Joyce, I can't go down there and pick out Ted's clothes and casket," she said.

"He was your husband, and that is your responsibility. Anyway, I do not think that is something I want to do," was my reply.

After much discussion, I finally gave in, with the condition she had to go with me and stand by my side as we finalized each step.

We walked down a flight of stairs into a room filled with caskets. Knowing Mother's situation, the director pointed out only ones that she could afford. We selected one from the row against the wall. I really didn't like being down there, but it had to be done. Mother stood by my side along with Bob, and we picked out a suit. I had never seen Ted in a suit, but it seemed important to Bob that he have one.

I said under my breath, "Well, I guess so—he didn't have to pay for it!" I wasn't very happy with Bob, and really didn't want him even involved in the decision-making. I also didn't want to cause any confusion because Mother was under a lot of stress, so I kept my mouth shut and looked straight ahead as if Bob wasn't even there.

We returned upstairs, went back into the director's office to finalize the arrangements, and turned to leave. The director called out to us to be back around three or four to view the body before the Receiving of Friends. We said goodbye and left for lunch. There was no need to drive home; that would mean a thirty-minute drive there and a thirty-minute drive back. Besides, I really didn't want to go back to that house. Anyway, Mother needed to buy some clothing, so we had an excuse to linger around town until it was time to view Ted's body.

Three o'clock couldn't arrive fast enough for me. I was tired and wanted to go home to rest. Junior should have arrived at the house by the time we returned from the funeral home, and hopefully he would stay with Mother so I could go home.

Mother and I ate lunch. Then we decided to walk up the street to the department store and purchase the items she needed. By the time we finished, it was time for us to go back and view the body. I wasn't looking forward to that at all. Surely Mother wouldn't ask me to do that also. Bob had said he would meet us back at the funeral home at three p.m. He could go back with Mother to view the body while I sat out front. At least, that was my thought.

When we arrived at the funeral home, Bob was nowhere to be found. Mother and I sat and waited for a while, but Bob never returned. After a short period, the funeral home director came out to get Mother. She turned and said, "You're going too, aren't you?"

I looked at her in disbelief, yet again, and replied, "I wasn't planning on going back."

"Joyce, I can't go back there by myself," she replied.

I didn't owe her anything, yet she required me to do everything. After all, she had not really done anything for me in my life that had not produced pain. How dare she? It was as though she had thrown hot water in my face. My feet wouldn't move in order for me to stand up from the chair. How could she ask me to go back there and view Ted's body?

My lips were quivering with desperation as thoughts of running once again entered my mind. Nevertheless, as she stood there looking at me with those pleading eyes, somehow compassion came out of my heart, and I slowly rose and started walking behind her. We entered the room where Ted was, and Mother broke down sobbing. I gently touched her back in compassion as she laid her head on my shoulder. I hugged her with all my might and said, "Everything will be all right." I really don't know where that compassion came from, except from the grace of God.

The funeral home director sat Mother down in a chair. He looked at me and asked, "Can you view the body and tell her he looks okay?"

Why me? I asked myself once again. However, I knew it had to be done, so I slowly stepped forward to examine the way they had dressed Ted. I stood there for a few minutes, thinking about how much he had hurt me and how much pain I had endured at his hands. Suddenly my thoughts were interrupted by the funeral home director's voice.

"Is everything okay?" he asked.

"Yes. Can I have a minute, please?" I replied. I stood there for a few more minutes, and then I heard a prayer come from my lips.

"God, help me to release and forgive him of all the hurt he inflicted on me. I need you to heal the wounds of unforgiveness that are ripping my life apart. Please, God, help me to forgive and move past the torment of life's pains," I pleaded. Tears filled my eyes as I felt in my heart another layer of unforgiveness being chipped away by the hands of God. Yet as I continued standing there, eyes fixed on his lifeless body, I felt a battle going on in my mind.

Ted was dead, and it brought me great pleasure to know he would never be able to inflict pain on anyone else. Even feeling some release after my plea to God, I was still not sure I could really forgive fully and completely let it all go. Tears streamed down my cheeks as I battled the thoughts that were in conflict within my mind.

Once again, I was interrupted by the voice of the funeral home director. "Is everything okay?" I wiped the tears of pain from my eyes before I turned to answer his question.

"Yes. Can we please return upstairs?"

I glanced at Mother, and she seemed composed enough to handle viewing the body. I asked if she would like to view Ted's body before we returned upstairs. She stepped forward with some hesitation. She gripped my hand so tightly that pain shot through my hand and arm. I endured the pain as I comforted her as much as I could. I know, beyond a shadow of doubt, that God gave me the strength, grace, and love to show her the compassion she needed to make it through that dreadful day in her life. That day started a new beginning of pushing past the crusty soil of unforgiveness. Little by little, I would be set free from a life of torment and shame.

Thoughts of how we all make mistakes entered my mind. Yes, the pain Ted had inflicted on me seemed more than I could bear then or forgive now. However, I was reminded that we as individuals think some sins are worse than others in our eyes, but God sees them all the same. It didn't seem really fair to me, but I remembered that we all have sinned. At some time or in some place, we have abused and offended someone, either in deed or word. I knew none of us were perfect, yet I still made excuses for myself while condemning others. I guess I was doing what the Bible called trying to take a splinter out of someone else's eyes, while I had a plank in my own. (Matthew 7:4-5, NKJV). I began to realize that day that I was still a prisoner. I knew that if I didn't push past the rest of the hurts, I would continue to build barriers around myself and my emotions. Those walls were not only protecting me, but also shutting out anyone who dared to build any type of relationship with me.

I had drawn a circle around myself for protection. However, I soon found out the circle had become a prison that kept me from having a fulfilled life, not only in relationships, but also the workplace. I was very suspicious of anyone who made advances to enter my inner life. The abuse had tormented my life, destroyed many relationships, and robbed me of many nights' sleep. The hatred born of yesterday's pain had eaten me alive for many years. All of this because of the sexual, physical, and mental abuse I had suffered.

I repeatedly told myself that I had a right to feel the way I did about everyone and every situation that did not fit into my circle. Yet God knew, in His great wisdom, that I would never truly be set free until I could find that completely forgiving spirit. I had turned some things loose. However, was I really willing to cry out for a complete healing? I knew for sure that under my own strength it would be impossible. Yet each day God seemed to carry me to another level of forgiveness. I knew with God all things were possible according to the Bible, however where your own life is concerned, it seems like a different story. Was I willing to turn all of this painful situation, which had become as much a part of my life as eating food and drinking water, into the hands of the forgiving, loving Father I heard so much about in church? After all, where was "God" all those many times

I was abused at the hands of the person I had thought would be the real father I was looking for?

I would soon realize that God was right where He had always been, and without His protective hands, I would have died at the hands of an evil man. However, there were times that I really wondered why God had spared my life. Many years later, that question would be answered.

CHAPTER 45

Graveside Deliverance

Everyone else went into the church after the end of the graveside service. They would wait inside until the grave was covered and then return. However, I remained behind at the grave site, standing a short distance from the men who were placing the dirt on the grave. I watched intently as they placed the last shovel of dirt over Ted's grave. Flashbacks of the pain he had caused made me feel very uncomfortable. Tears once again filled my eyes. It is funny how memories of a painful event can enter your mind and seem as if they happened just yesterday. Fresh was the fear that had gripped my life for so many years. My chest felt tight, and my breathing seemed labored. I wanted to run as far away as possible to escape the feelings of fear, pain, and shame.

I began to shake and tremble as I stared at the grave. Would the fear and anxiety I had carried for what seemed a lifetime ever be completely gone? Would I be chased by the tormenting dreams of the past? Would I ever be released from the grip that seemed to hold my mind, heart, and soul? *Just run and never look back*, repeated in my mind like a car going 150 miles per hour around and around on a race track. However, my feet were frozen to the ground and my eyes were glued to the grave site. Thoughts of what I said many years ago echoed through my mind. "I hope I see you burning in hell someday." Now that was not as important. It seemed that each shovel of dirt that was placed on the grave diminished my pain Would I be able, at last, to move forward with my life?

My thoughts were interrupted by Mother's voice. "Joyce, are you okay?"

I turned and looked at a pale, aging face full of sadness and stress. "Yes, I am just making sure they place the flowers correctly," I replied.

She walked closer and placed her arms around my waist. I pulled away, pretending I was placing one of the flower arrangements in a better place. I reached over, pulled out a rose from the family arrangement, handed to her, and said, "I need to go home. Junior said he was spending the night with you, so he will take you home."

"Okay. Please call me when you get there," she replied.

As I slowly turned to walk away, the sun was peeking over the tree tops as if to say, "This is a new day with many brighter tomorrows. Use them wisely and make each day a day that will count for your life, the life of your family, and a deeper relationship with your Heavenly Father." Walking to my car, I said goodbye to another layer of pain. Once again, I would drive away, but this time was different. I knew in my heart that I would not have doubts and fears lingering in my heart about Ted. For some reason, I stopped the car and looked back. I could see the tent that covered his grave as the sun gleamed against the backdrop of trees that lay behind the graveyard. I turned and looked through the rearview mirror. I pressed the gas pedal and watched the tent fade out of sight as I rounded the curve in the road.

It was over! This time there was no fear of Ted causing me any more pain. However, would that be the end of a painful story? Had I really been set free by a few shovels of dirt? Would I be able to sleep in peace, without the dreams of yesterday's pain invading my life? Only God and time would tell. Nevertheless, that day I knew something had changed in my life. My feelings of hatred for Ted weren't as deep as they had been before. As I drove home that late afternoon, tears streamed down my face. Was it because Ted was dead? No, it was because I felt a little less pain in my heart from my past abuse. The tears that flowed were a release of past hurts and a new beginning for me. As I drove, I felt deep down in my heart God's voice speaking to me. His voice said, "Joyce, let it go."

I knew at that moment that with God's help, I could continue the process of peeling off a layer at a time of pain, fear, and shame. Did all this happen overnight? Absolutely not! But little by little, I could see myself coming out of the feelings of worthlessness into a new life with a new beginning. Even when my heart and spirit were broken, God was there to lift me up with His healing hands. The miraculous love of God is the only way I could see to get past the pain and find a new level of strength and courage to continue the healing process. Life is not always fair, in our eyes, but there is always a path from the dark side of the desert to the light of a brighter tomorrow, if we will forgive through God's unconditional love. Deliverance for me was a work in process. Nevertheless, I have had many more brighter tomorrows in my life since I opened my heart to God's healing hands.

Deborah and I fully forgave Mother for the rejection and abandonment we felt as children. She is very sick at this time, and doctors have given her only six months to live. Deborah and I have cared for Mother and made sure she is comfortable in her last days as if nothing negative happened between us in the past. We both are sad to see her frail, sick, and broken, but we did answer the call to help her through these difficult times without regrets. We want to walk in the true love that God's word talks about.

CHAPTER 46

Brighter Tomorrows

Many of us have been wounded and are dealing with pain and suffering. It may be a family member, a friend, or a stranger who abused and hurt us. We may not be able to have a relationship with the one who abused us. In my case I could not, and I do not believe God expected me to have a relationship with someone whom I could not trust because of the many times he had broken that trust through abuse. However, I do believe that God expects us to forgive. You may not have to take the journey I did, because you don't have to be face-to-face with your abuser to forgive them. Forgiveness takes place between you and God.

It took a long time for me to understand that concept. Forgiveness is a heart change that produces light where there is darkness. Through forgiveness, you can walk forward into a new life that is filled with many, many new beginnings. God does offer new hope of a brighter tomorrow through forgiveness. How do I know that? Because I have experienced first-hand how forgiveness can set you free and bring you into a new beginning filled with God's love. Forgiveness is a work in progress. Progress means you are advancing forward or to a higher journey. As long as we are moving forward, we are making progress.

But wasn't what they did wrong? Yes, yes, yes! Forgiving speaks the truth to what happened. It calls bad things bad. However, we must get past our hurt and stop clinging to the self-pity to which we have become accustomed. The offenders are guilty. They don't deserve to be forgiven, but by the love of God and by His grace we find a way to forgive. The sooner we face up to the fact that we all have shortcomings, the sooner the healing process can begin. God says in His Word that He forgives the past, present, and future sins. That means God is always forgiving us. We need to let God deal with those who have hurt us. Even in those darkest moments of my life, somehow God's loving power brought me toward a life of restoration, a life of serving Him, a life of encouragement, and a life of brighter tomorrows.

I still had many bumps in the road I had to overcome. So will you! There will be hills to climb and bumpy railroads to cross. However, life isn't about waiting for the storms to pass; it's about learning to dance in the rain while we wait for God to guide us down the road of forgiveness and restoration. He is a loving God and what was meant for evil, He will turn to good—if we will let go and let Him guide us into a new day of forgiveness. Second Corinthians 12:9a says, "And He said to me, "My grace is sufficient for you, for My strength is made perfect in weakness" (NKJV). As we all go down the many roads of life, we cannot see far without God's wisdom. However, our weakness is made perfect in God's strength. Today, start your process of forgiveness and watch God bring new beginnings into your life day by day. You'll be glad you did!

She Has Gone Home

As I was writing the finishing touches on this book, Mother took a turn for the worse. The six months they said she had left ended up being only two months. Mother has gone home to her Heavenly Father. I didn't think I could sit by her bed and hold her hand while she took her last breath, but somehow, like all those years before, God gave me the strength to see her through until the end. Deborah, Junior, and I spent the last week of Mother's life by her side praying, reading the Bible, and comforting her in any way we could. Deborah, my son, and I watched as Mother took her last breath and peacefully crossed from this world to her new home in heaven. You could feel the Angels in her room waiting to escort her to the arms of her Heavenly Father. It was like nothing I had ever experienced before. She left knowing that she was loved by her children and that everything that had happened in the past was forgiven. I will always remember my mother in a loving way and will see her when my time comes to cross over to my Heavenly home. She is waiting to welcome all of us home. Our mother is in her brighter tomorrows.

Chapter 47

Word of Wisdom for Those Who Are Being Abused

(Seek Help and Protection)

My hope is that those who read this book will find encouragement in facing a life of forgiveness. First and foremost, you will need to forgive yourself. You have done nothing wrong to be the recipient of this abuse. Many abusers will try to make you feel you have done something to deserve this pain. (That was one of the first things I had to deal with.) Not so! If you are experiencing sexual, physical, or verbal abuse at the hand of anyone, I plead with you to seek help and protection from the abuser. *Do not* stay in the situation because of fear! God never ordained abuse, and he does not want you to be abused. The biggest mistake I made was staying because of fear. No one should control your life in this manner, nor should you be willing to continue to be the object of their abuse because of insecurities and sins in their own life. I repeatedly confronted Mother with the fact that I was being abused. However, she chose to turn a blind eye to all that was taking place in her own home. If you are being abused and are experiencing the same results with a family member that I did, you must seek protection outside of the home!

You are a wonderful, beautiful person in the eyes of a loving God. For many years, I felt guilty and walked in condemnation. Don't let anyone ever tell you that you are worthless, ugly, poor, and deserve what you are receiving. Never let fear hold you back or cause you to stay in an abusive situation. God has created in all of us the potential to rise above our circumstances and move forward into a life of forgiving love. It was not easy for me, and it took many years of peeling away yesterday's pains and hurts before I could totally be set free. It may also take you many years to do the same, but it will be worth all the time spent in prayer and reading His Word to be set free.

Against all worldly odds, I rose out of a life of condemnation, negativity, abuse, and rejection. What the world meant for evil, God used for His good. I am no longer a product of my past, but a witness of how God can peel away each layer of hurt and pain, one layer at a time, until we have been completely set free. However, until we take that first step into a path of healing at the hands of a loving God, we will never experience the kind of peace that it talks about in His Word. Philippians 4:7 says, "And the peace of God, which surpasses all understanding, will guard your hearts and minds through Christ Jesus" (NKJV)."

Take the first step into a new day of loving yourself as much as God loves you. "You are made in His image and likeness," the Bible says. You have nothing to be ashamed of. God is not looking at your past, but the future you and He can build together. God loves you right where you are and is waiting with open arms to help you start your new journey. There will be some setbacks. However, if you will keep your eyes on the future and not on the past, one day you will wake up and the memory of yesterday's pains and hurts will be less invasive in your mind, thoughts, and life. Somehow they will fade away, little by little, as you come to see yourself as God sees you, and not as the world sees you or even how you see yourself.

We must always remember that God only wants the best for us. It is the enemy who seeks to destroy your life. When evil enters the heart of man, it is then that Satan uses him to steal and destroy not only his own life, but also those around him. John 10:10 says, "The thief (Satan) does not come except to steal, and kill, and destroy. I (Jesus) have come that they may have life, and that they may have it more abundantly"(NKJV).

God has worked miracle after miracle in my life. However, that didn't happen until I was willing to give Him control of my life and future. God does not respect any of us over the other (Acts 10:34 and Deuteronomy 10:17, NKJV). What He did for me, He will also do for you. My family, my church, my school, and the world marked me off as a lost cause. However, God saw in me what no one else could see or imagine. He gave me the ability to become a productive, caring individual who learned how to forgive, even in the face of a destructive force that loomed over my life trying to destroy any chance of a normal life. I rose above the circumstances that tormented me for years and stepped into a future of blessings that I could never have dreamed of seeing. God has restored many times over what was lacking or robbed from me in my childhood and in my teenage years. He said in His Word that He would restore what the canker-worm (locust) had destroyed. (Joel 2:25, NKJV) Ask God to restore every place in your life that has been broken.

The world had marked me as a child without a future, and some may say that about you. Nevertheless, God stepped into my upside-down world and turned my life right-side-up into a life of serving Him. Only God and you can determine your future! Don't ever let anyone tell you that you will not amount to anything in this world. God used a donkey to talk to a man and change his course of life (Numbers 22: 22–31, NKJV) He also can use us to bring healing to a hurting world.

I am living proof that God can and will change your life and take you down a path to help others to be set free. You can choose to remain in the same routine of a destructive lifestyle, or you can move forward with the help of His healing hands. However, you must take the first step in walking forward into a forgiving life, a love for yourself, and a willingness to seek God's healing hand. He is ready to start the healing process! How many times does God say to forgive your brother? Matthew 18:21–22 says, "Then Peter came to Him and said, 'Lord how often shall my brother sin against me, and I forgive him? Up to seven times?' Jesus said to him, 'I do not say to you, up to seven times, but up to seventy times seven'" (NKJV). Jesus did not give a mathematical formula. He means limitless forgiveness. He forgives all of us each day of our lives when we come to Him and ask forgiveness for our sins. In other words, God forgives us continually. We cannot ask of someone else what we are not willing to give.

Today, you can start a renewed life in Christ and move forward on your journey of forgiveness. The choice is yours! You truly have nothing to lose and much to gain if you move with God's Spirit and wisdom. Yield to the "Great Counselor" and you will never regret letting God sweep away all the pain, hurt, and rejections that have tormented you for many years. Matthew 11:28–29 says, "Come to Me, all you who labor and are heavy laden, and I will give you rest. Take My yoke upon you and learn from

Me, for I am gentle and lowly in heart, and you will find rest for your souls" (NKJV).

It was difficult to bridge the distance between Roger, Mother, Grandpa and Grandma Smith and I because of the rejection and pain I felt they had inflicted on me. However, as I look back, I know that God had a plan for me even then. When I read the scripture in Jeremiah 1:5, "Before I formed you in the womb I knew you; before you were born I sanctified you; I ordained you" (NKJV), I know that my God knew what he was doing before He formed me in my mother's womb. I was not a mistake, nor was I an accident. He knew who I was. He had sanctified me and ordained me for His work even before I was born. If God knew Jeremiah, He also knew me. I knew there had to be hope emerging from a stormy night of rejection in the womb for this little country girl.

None of us are mistakes. God will raise us up into a life that will glorify Him, if we will move forward with His guidance and plan. Remember, God knew you before you were formed in the womb. He has a plan for your life! Yesterday's sorrows can become today's and tomorrow's rewards through the hands of an almighty God. With God's help, we can always turn a lemon-sour life into a pitcher of sweet lemonade. Yesterday's pain and sorrows became a stepping stone for a better life, personally and in Christ, for the blue eyed, blond-headed country girl who was told she didn't have a future. No matter what emotional storm you have encountered, don't cave into those emotions. Be encouraged! God is reaching out with His healing hand to help you start your journey to a better tomorrow. Place your trust in God, for it has been proven that He is absolutely trustworthy. Are you ready to start your new journey? Step out of the darkness of unforgiveness and into the light with a forgiving spirit of love and you will find that you are the one who has been truly set free. The next move is yours!

Manufactured By: RR Donnelley
                     Breinigsville, PA USA
                     February, 2011